Support, Transmission, Education and Target Varieties in the Celtic Languages

Like many languages across the globe, the Celtic languages today are experiencing varying degrees of minoritisation and revitalisation. The experience of the Celtic languages in the twenty-first century is characterised by language shift to English and French, but they have also been the focus of official and grassroots initiatives aimed at reinvigorating the minoritised languages. This modern reality is evident in the profile of contemporary users of the Celtic languages, in the type of variation that they practise, and in their views on Celtic language and society in the twenty-first century. In turn, this reality provides a challenge to preconceived ideas about what the Celtic languages are like and how they should be regarded and managed at local and global levels.

This book aims to shed light on some of the main issues facing the Celtic languages into the future and to showcase different approaches to studying such contexts. It presents contributions interested in explicating the modern condition of the Celtic languages. It engages with attitudinal support for the Celtic languages, modes of language transmission, choosing educational models in minority settings, pedagogical approaches for language learners and perceptions of linguistic practices. These issues are considered within the context of language shift and revitalisation in the Celtic languages.

The chapters in this book were originally published as a special issue of *Language, Culture and Curriculum*.

Noel Ó Murchadha is Assistant Professor in Language Education at Trinity College Dublin, Ireland. He teaches courses on bi/multilingualism, language pedagogy and research methods in language and education. His research focuses on attitudes and ideologies on linguistic variation, especially in minority contexts. He has completed projects on teenagers' and educators' perceptions of linguistic variation in Irish and on language standardisation. His work examines the changing relationship between self and society in late modernity and the impact that such changes have on language variation and change in minoritised contexts.

Bettina Migge is Professor of Linguistics and Head of the School of Languages, Cultures and Linguistics at University College Dublin, Ireland. She is a member of the research group CNRS-SeDyL (France). She teaches courses in sociolinguistics and contact linguistics and has published extensively on diachronic and synchronic language contact, language variation and change, language documentation in multilingual contexts focusing on lesser-used languages and on identity formation in contexts of migration. Empirically, her research has focused on the Creoles of Suriname and French Guiana, the Gbe languages (Benin) and more recently on Irish English.

Support, Transmission, Education and Target Varieties in the Celtic Languages

Edited by
Noel Ó Murchadha and Bettina Migge

LONDON AND NEW YORK

First published 2018
by Routledge
2 Park Square, Milton Park, Abingdon, Oxon, OX14 4RN, UK

and by Routledge
711 Third Avenue, New York, NY 10017, USA

Routledge is an imprint of the Taylor & Francis Group, an informa business

© 2018 Taylor & Francis

All rights reserved. No part of this book may be reprinted or reproduced or utilised in any form or by any electronic, mechanical, or other means, now known or hereafter invented, including photocopying and recording, or in any information storage or retrieval system, without permission in writing from the publishers.

Trademark notice: Product or corporate names may be trademarks or registered trademarks, and are used only for identification and explanation without intent to infringe.

British Library Cataloguing in Publication Data
A catalogue record for this book is available from the British Library

ISBN13: 978-1-138-49839-6

Typeset in MyriadPro
by diacriTech, Chennai

Publisher's Note
The publisher accepts responsibility for any inconsistencies that may have arisen during the conversion of this book from journal articles to book chapters, namely the possible inclusion of journal terminology.

Disclaimer
Every effort has been made to contact copyright holders for their permission to reprint material in this book. The publishers would be grateful to hear from any copyright holder who is not here acknowledged and will undertake to rectify any errors or omissions in future editions of this book.

Contents

Citation Information		vii
Notes on Contributors		ix
	Introduction: Support, transmission, education and target varieties in the Celtic languages: an overview *Noel Ó Murchadha and Bettina Migge*	1
1	Celtic languages and sociolinguistics: a very brief overview of pertinent issues *John Edwards*	13
2	'Is it really for talking?': the implications of associating a minority language with the school *Cassie Smith-Christmas*	32
3	Factors influencing the likelihood of choice of Gaelic-medium primary education in Scotland: results from a national public survey *Fiona O'Hanlon and Lindsay Paterson*	48
4	Developing resources for translanguaging in minority language contexts: A case study of rapping in an Irish primary school *Máiréad Moriarty*	76
5	Finding an ideological niche for new speakers in a minoritised language community *Michael Hornsby*	91
	Index	105

Citation Information

The chapters in this book were originally published in *Language, Culture and Curriculum*, volume 30, issue 1 (March 2017). When citing this material, please use the original page numbering for each article, as follows:

Introduction
Support, transmission, education and target varieties in the Celtic languages: an overview
Noel Ó Murchadha and Bettina Migge
Language, Culture and Curriculum, volume 30, issue 1 (March 2017) pp. 1–12

Chapter 1
Celtic languages and sociolinguistics: a very brief overview of pertinent issues
John Edwards
Language, Culture and Curriculum, volume 30, issue 1 (March 2017) pp. 13–31

Chapter 2
'Is it really for talking?': the implications of associating a minority language with the school
Cassie Smith-Christmas
Language, Culture and Curriculum, volume 30, issue 1 (March 2017) pp. 32–47

Chapter 3
Factors influencing the likelihood of choice of Gaelic-medium primary education in Scotland: results from a national public survey
Fiona O'Hanlon and Lindsay Paterson
Language, Culture and Curriculum, volume 30, issue 1 (March 2017) pp. 48–75

Chapter 4
Developing resources for translanguaging in minority language contexts: A case study of rapping in an Irish primary school
Máiréad Moriarty
Language, Culture and Curriculum, volume 30, issue 1 (March 2017) pp. 76–90

CITATION INFORMATION

Chapter 5

Finding an ideological niche for new speakers in a minoritized language community
Michael Hornsby
Language, Culture and Curriculum, volume 30, issue 1 (March 2017) pp. 91–104

For any permission-related enquiries please visit:
http://www.tandfonline.com/page/help/permissions

Notes on Contributors

John Edwards is Professor of Psychology at St. Francis Xavier University, Nova Scotia, Canada. His research has been interdisciplinary within educational theory, linguistics, social psychology and political science, and has centred on multilingualism, identity, ethnicity, nationalism and language. His recent publications include *Minority Languages and Group Identity* (2010), *Challenges in the Social Life of Language* (2011) and *Multilingualism: Understanding Linguistic Diversity* (2012).

Michael Hornsby is Professor in the Centre for Celtic Studies at Adam Mickiewicz University, Poznań, Poland. His research interests focus on sociolinguistics and linguistic anthropology, especially the reaction of speech communities to the pressures of globalisation and modernisation. He is also interested in the preservation, revitalisation and transformation of minority languages, and language authenticity. He is the author of *Revitalizing Minority Languages: New Speakers of Breton, Yiddish and Lemko* (2015).

Bettina Migge is Professor of Linguistics and Head of the School of Languages, Cultures and Linguistics at University College Dublin, Ireland. She is a member of the research group CNRS-SeDyL (France). She teaches courses in sociolinguistics and contact linguistics and has published extensively on diachronic and synchronic language contact, language variation and change, language documentation in multilingual contexts focusing on lesser-used languages and on identity formation in contexts of migration. Empirically, her research has focused on the Creoles of Suriname and French Guiana, the Gbe languages (Benin) and more recently on Irish English.

Máiréad Moriarty is a Lecturer in Sociolinguistics, and Assistant Dean (International) in the Faculty of Arts, Humanities and Social Sciences at the University of Limerick, Ireland. Her research focuses on the relationship between language and society, particularly on the representation of language and language varieties in the media and in the study of minority language policy and planning. She is the author of *Globalizing Language Policy and Planning: An Irish Language Perspective* (2015).

Fiona O'Hanlon is Chancellor's Fellow in Languages Education at the University of Edinburgh, UK. Her research is interested in language and equity issues, and how these are taken forward in education and educational policy. Her current projects include an investigation of Gaelic-medium teachers' views of the pedagogical practice of

NOTES ON CONTRIBUTORS

translanguaging, and a comparative study of the language use, identities, and patterns of civic participation of young people who are in Gaelic-medium or Welsh-medium education or are learning Gaelic or Welsh in secondary school.

Noel Ó Murchadha is Assistant Professor in Language Education at Trinity College Dublin, Ireland. He teaches courses on bi/multilingualism, language pedagogy and research methods in language and education. His research focuses on attitudes and ideologies on linguistic variation, especially in minority contexts. He has completed projects on teenagers' and educators' perceptions of linguistic variation in Irish and on language standardisation. His work examines the changing relationship between self and society in late modernity and the impact that such changes have on language variation and change in minoritised contexts.

Lindsay Paterson is Professor of Education Policy in the School of Social and Political Science at the University of Edinburgh, UK. His work focuses on five main areas: twentieth-century educational reform, the long-term effects of educational reform, the effect of education on civic values, educational expansion and social mobility and the status of Gaelic in Scotland. He is the author of *Social Radicalism and Liberal Education* (2015).

Cassie Smith-Christmas is a postdoctoral Fellow at the University of Limerick, Ireland, and is conducting a comparative study of Family Language Policy in Scotland and Ireland. She was previously a research fellow for Soillse, the interuniversity Gaelic language research network, for the University of the Highlands and Islands. She is the author of *Family Language Policy: Maintaining an Endangered Language in the Home* (2016).

INTRODUCTION

Support, transmission, education and target varieties in the Celtic languages: an overview

Introduction

When we talk of the modern Celtic languages today, we refer to the Insular[1] Celtic varieties that have maintained (or indeed regained) a degree of their linguistic vitality and that are practised, to varying extents and in various forms, by users of the Breton, Cornish, Irish, Manx, Scottish Gaelic and Welsh languages. Further to their common linguistic derivation, the Celtic languages share a number of additional characteristics that lend themselves well to a common analytical framework (features that they indeed share with many other 'small' languages). Each of the languages has, for a long time, been functioning in a bilingual, if not multilingual, environment (e.g. Timm, 2009, 2013, on Breton; Ferdinand, 2013; George & Broderick, 2009, on Cornish; Doyle, 2015; Mac-Giolla Chriost, 2005, on Irish; George & Broderick, 2009, on Manx; Ó Baoill, 2010; Watson and MacLeod, 2010 on Scottish Gaelic; Davies, 2014, on Welsh). Contact with major global languages has had a decisive and formative effect on the trajectories of the Celtic languages (cf. chapters in Tristram, 2007). The reality of interaction with the French and English languages since the sixteenth century and especially in more recent centuries has meant that the Celtic languages have been subject to historical processes of minoritisation and language shift (Fife, 2009; Price, 1992). Consequently, in global terms, each of the languages is reliant on a relatively small pool of speakers for their survival. Perhaps unsurprisingly for those familiar with the dynamics of minority languages, then, language maintenance, revitalisation and revival projects have been among of the hallmarks of the Celtic language experience for some time. This speaks to a familiar appetite among at least some users, as well as non-users, to go against the grain of language loss and to try to ensure that the Celtic languages are used into the future despite an extremely challenging climate.

This special issue of *Language, Culture and Curriculum* emerged from the first Celtic Sociolinguistics Symposium held at University College Dublin in June 2015. The Symposium, in turn, focused on themes that permeate research on the sociolinguistics of the Celtic languages, including intergenerational transmission; language and identity; language in education; language in the media and attitudes to linguistic variation. The investigation of sociolinguistic aspects of the Celtic languages provides a useful pan-Celtic perspective on issues in other languages that are endangered and have benefited from revitalisation activities. It thus lends itself to the analysis of the relationship between language and society in related, yet diverse, spaces and cultures. Of course, any sociolinguistic account of the Celtic languages, in one way or another, has to deal with issues of language endangerment and language revival. Therefore, in addition to advancing our understanding of the Celtic languages, the study of their current status offers a context-specific window into the dynamics of minoritised languages and language varieties in modern Western society. The study of the Celtic languages and their speakers can, in this way, illuminate the social, cultural and political factors that shape processes of language loss and preservation. It thus has the potential to enhance our understanding of how social actors recruit, or, perhaps more pertinently in some cases, do not recruit, minority languages in negotiating increasingly fluid social, cultural and political environments. In addition, it adds to our understanding of both language and society in a globalised world. Following a brief outline of speaker demographics in the next section, the remainder of this introductory article will focus on some of the key issues currently faced by the Celtic languages and will illustrate how this special issue makes a contribution to scholarship in those areas.

Speaker demographics

The worldwide trend of diminishing linguistic diversity is well documented (e.g. Crystal, 2000; Dorian, 2014; Moseley, 2012; Nettle & Romaine, 2000) and the Celtic languages are, or have historically been, subject to the global flows that induce and precipitate language shift. Intergenerational transmission in the home is routinely cited as one of the mainstays of successful initiatives to sustain the vigour of threatened languages or to reverse processes of language shift (Fishman, 1991). The low level, or in some cases the complete collapse, of transfer of the Celtic languages in the home has significantly contributed to shaping the current status of the languages, however (e.g. Jones, 1998; McLeod, 2014; Ó Giollagáin & Charlton, 2015). Likewise, the interaction between the home domain and other linguistically strategic domains has impacted language vitality in the Celtic varieties. Consequently, reported total numbers of speakers of the Celtic languages today and the geographical distribution of those speakers sketch a very different picture from times when the languages were in their pomp. Data on user numbers, despite their limitations and the variation in the levels of detail available in the different language contexts, provide a useful view of the extent of the languages in the different polities where they are primarily used. The data on the Gaelic varieties (Irish, Scottish Gaelic and Manx) tell us that in Ireland, over 77,000 speakers report speaking Irish on a daily basis outside the education system in the Republic of Ireland (Central Statistics Office, 2012), while in Northern Ireland, just under 98,000 people claim an ability to speak Irish (Northern Ireland Statistics & Research Agency, 2012). The figures for Scottish Gaelic reveal that in excess of 57,000 people in Scotland claim an ability to speak the language (National Records of Scotland, 2015) with others claiming 'Gaelic languages', as their 'mother tongue' in Canada (Statistics Canada, 2012). In terms of Manx, more than 1600 claim an ability to speak the language (Economic Affairs Division, Isle of Man Government Treasury, 2012) while in the case of Welsh, almost 361,000 people in Wales report using the language on a daily basis (Welsh Government & Welsh Language Commissioner, 2015) with further speakers present in Patagonia, Argentina (Jones, 2012). Although the last native speaker of Cornish is both widely and contentiously reported to have died in the late eighteenth century, some 500 individuals returned as Cornish speakers in the 2011 UK Census (Office for National Statistics, 2013), despite there being no designated space on the form to do so (Tresidder, 2015, p. 217). In Brittany, at the same time, approximately 200,000 speakers of Breton are estimated (Ofis Publik ar Brezhoneg, 2013).

Owing to the loss of domains of usage, as witnessed in the relatively weak patterns of intergenerational transmission in the home and in patterns of peer and community language usage, the Celtic languages are today much more heavily reliant on alternative modes of language transmission and on the interaction between the home and other domains in order to sustain the individual languages. This is the reality faced in supporting the Celtic varieties both in those areas where they endure as community varieties (with a range of degrees of robustness) and in facilitating the expansion of the pool of users beyond these areas. The academic literature on minority language communities commonly reveals that maintenance efforts face challenges in terms of fostering support for small languages, in relation to language transmission in the home, in defining the role of education in maintenance, revitalisation and revival and in establishing the target language variety/varieties. The Celtic languages are no exception. These issues will each be discussed in turn below with a view to mapping how scholarship on the sociolinguistics of the Celtic languages might progress in the future.

Fostering support

The loss of status and prestige has historically had a decisive impact on the fate of the Celtic languages (Price, 1992), as has been the case in language minoritisation worldwide (Fishman, 1991). The advance of English and French and their dominance in prestige domains was accompanied by an inverse development in the Celtic varieties. The Celtic languages gradually came to be deemed superfluous, perhaps even detrimental, to economic progress and social mobility in their respective polities. In modern times, where users of the Celtic languages are at least bilingual, the way the languages are perceived remains important. Positive perceptions of the communicative and the symbolic functions of the languages are fundamental to their continued use in the future. Where individuals raised in Celtic language-speaking homes/communities are convinced of the continued utility of the languages in their own lives, it follows that they are more likely to remain active users of the languages. Likewise for new speakers who have acquired high degrees of proficiency in the languages. For learners or potential learners, the perceived integrative and instrumental value of the Celtic varieties will play an important role in motivating them to commit themselves to attaining a level of ability that will allow them to function in the languages. Even among non-users, the perception of the Celtic languages is important so that resources dedicated to them can be justified with reference to existing levels of public support for their continued use. Support for maintaining the Celtic languages is evident in attitudinal research (e.g. Darmody & Daly, 2015; Mac Gréil & Rhatigan, 2009), in the continued use of the languages by some members of traditional communities, in the commitment of new speakers to the languages and in the appetite of some non-users to learn the languages. However, it is unclear to what extent the current levels of support will secure their futures. How the languages are perceived remains important in deciding their future, but it remains unclear what the conditions are under which support for the Celtic languages translates to actual increases in usage or language transmission. This is a question that would benefit from more sustained sociolinguistic attention. In outlining the current state of play, John Edwards, in his article in this special issue, assesses some of the primary challenges faced by the Celtic languages and thus contributes to this debate.

SUPPORT, TRANSMISSION, EDUCATION AND TARGET VARIETIES

In a broad-ranging article, Edwards examines the current status and future trajectories of the Celtic languages. Focusing especially, though not exclusively, on the Irish and Scottish Gaelic contexts, he explores the factors that continue to restrict the maintenance and expansion of the Celtic languages. Based mainly on a critical assessment of recent media reports on Celtic languages, Edwards shows that the continued use and, particularly, the expansion of the Celtic languages is hampered by negative attitudes in wider society and by the fact that the Celtic languages are still underrepresented in the public sphere. Celtic languages, for instance, are rarely able to occupy a discursive space on their own, but typically coexist with the dominant language in the setting in order to cater to the needs of the majority population who normally have, at best, a passive knowledge of these languages. Although, he argues, there continues to be sufficient enthusiasm among the wider population and policy-makers to maintain some measures to promote these languages, provisions such as Celtic language-medium education are generally only partially effective. He contends that there is generally either a lack of 'man power', such as the absence of qualified teachers to properly carry out these measures or there is a lack of funding. Overall, the situation, he suggests, makes for a rather bleak future.

Language transmission

Supporters of the Celtic languages face challenges in assuring the public of the merits of communicating in these languages and of making available financial and human resources to support their survival (e.g. Darmody & Daly, 2015; Edwards, this issue; Mac Gréil & Rhatigan, 2009). A significant cohort, however, are already committed to maintaining, revitalising or reviving Breton, Cornish, Scottish Gaelic, Irish, Manx and Welsh. Many are aware of the benefits of a form of bilingualism that incorporates a Celtic language, are committed to using the language, and/or desire and plan for the next generation to have an ability to communicate in a Celtic language. The choice of language management strategies to achieve transmission to the next generation, however, does not always align with documented successful models (e.g. Ó hlfearnáin, 2006; O'Toole & Hickey, 2016; Smith-Christmas, this issue). Examples are thus described in the literature of situations where even caregivers who are highly competent in one of the Celtic languages and who wish for their children to be skilled bilinguals do not maximise exposure to the minority language in the home (Ó hlfearnáin, 2006; Smith-Christmas, this issue). Furthermore, the way these minoritised varieties are used, not used or discursively framed in the home can engender links between the languages and other domains, such as education or religion, in a way that confines them to those domains and renders their use in the broader context highly marked (Smith-Christmas, 2014, this issue). A mismatch between language management strategies and desired outcomes is evident and is largely attributable to insufficient awareness of successful models of language transmission or to the difficulties in implementing such models despite awareness of them. Although sociolinguists working on the Celtic languages have, with large degrees of success, identified the factors influencing language abandonment, the message regarding strategies for successful transmission in the home has not fully filtered down to the grassroots level. Celtic sociolinguists' proclivity for pointing to the (albeit important) tell tales of language decline, to the neglect of comprehensive descriptions of successful language transmission strategies in the home, is noteworthy here. While the abundant literature that describes the conditions of shift in the Celtic languages is illuminating, only a very sparse literature exists recounting the, admittedly more scarce, examples of successful Celtic language transmission in the home. The academic endeavour to comprehensively outline language shift, maintenance, revitalisation and revival, as well as the general public concerned with the fate of the Celtic varieties, would benefit from scholars becoming more *engagé* in cases of successful transmission. Such a development would advance our understanding of the conditions of small languages and, in addition, provide an exemplar for the converted. The article in this special issue by Cassie Smith-Christmas falls within this area.

The discursive framing of the Celtic languages among their speakers and its impact on language maintenance is the topic of the article by Smith-Christmas. The article critically investigates a long-standing issue that exists in minority language maintenance, namely how minority language immersion programmes and the broader community interact and whether or not the relationship between the two is conducive to the continued vitality of the minority language. Based on an analysis of data from long-term participant observation and recordings of language practices in an extended Scottish Gaelic-speaking family on the Isle of Skye, Smith-Christmas shows that the lack of use of Scottish Gaelic outside of the educational context is not solely attributable to a lack of competence in the language. Rather, it is contended that patterns of language usage are moulded by the language practices of caregivers and the strategies that they employ in order to encourage the use of Gaelic in the youngest generation. The micro-interactional analysis shows that despite the fact that the caregivers of the child in the study, Maggie, generally have highly positive views of Gaelic, are themselves active users of the language, and are in favour of passing it on, Gaelic is not always the medium of interaction between adults in front of the child and child-directed uses of Gaelic are generally framed as a pedagogical exercise. As a result, the author suggests that Maggie has internalised the view that Gaelic is only available for irregular, school-based interaction. In light of this, it seems that despite the desire to achieve language transmission in the home, the fate of the Celtic varieties may be largely dependent on the education system, a point that will be elaborated now.

The role of education

The presence of minoritised languages in education, whether subject only, bilingual programmes, or a full immersion experience, is mostly viewed in a positive light by those interested in their preservation, although it is by no means the panacea that some enthusiasts hope for (e.g. chapters in Hornberger, 2008). Much of what emerges from sociolinguistic research on the effectiveness of language education in the Celtic varieties highlights the many strengths of these initiatives and, especially, the challenges they face. The significant demand that exists for education in the Celtic languages (Darmody & Daly, 2015; O'Hanlon & Patterson, this issue; Redknap, 2006) suggests that educational models that include them either as a subject or as a medium of instruction are recognised as effective for linguistic development and/or for broader educational success. Education in the Celtic varieties undoubtedly has the potential as well as a documented record of developing learners' language proficiency (McCloskey, 2001; Nance, 2015; Ó Duibhir, 2009) of moulding positive ideologies around the languages (McCloskey, 2001; Walsh & O'Rourke, 2014) and of functioning as a trigger that prompts lifelong participation in the ethnoculture of habitual users of the languages (Walsh & O'Rourke, 2014). However, the modern history of the institutionalisation of the Celtic languages in the form of educational provision demonstrates that the rollout of language in education programmes, even full immersion models, does not guarantee a vibrant language community (Dunmore, 2014). If it were the case that the inclusion of the Celtic languages in education resulted in widespread use of the languages beyond that domain, for instance, languages like Welsh and Irish (which have a relatively strong presence in education) would be far more widely practised outside education than is presently the case.

The myriad factors influencing the choice or potential choice to study a Celtic language or to study through the medium of a Celtic language tend to vary. They include, for example, attitudinal factors, a desire to ensure that children develop linguistic proficiency in a Celtic variety, the alignment with a particular culture or identity, and in some cases, an elitist desire to avoid alternatives due to the socio-economic profiles of students (Baker, 2000; Kavanagh, 2013; Mas-Moury Mack, 2013; O'Hanlon, 2015). People also foreground instrumental reasons such as the pursuit of the academic success that is associated with education in a language that is not the home language and the educational benefits that are linked to bilingualism (Baker, 2000; Kavanagh, 2013; Mas-Moury Mack, 2013; O'Hanlon, 2015). But, there are also other, more mundane, reasons that play a role such as a school's proximity to the home or to work. Just as the factors that influence the decision to seek education in a Celtic language vary, so does the support for the Celtic language outside of school. Support in the form of opportunities for language use and for the development of literacy in the Celtic languages, for example, is available for some students through the community and in the home, yet is not accessible to others. It is hardly a shock, then, that student outcomes vary with regard to linguistic proficiency and language ideologies, and that education does not lead to more widespread use of the languages outside that domain. Students' motivation to engage with the languages clearly plays an important role.

Owing to the diverse sociolinguistic profiles and motivations of students developing proficiency in the Celtic languages through subject only or through Celtic language-medium education (e.g. Baker, 2000; Hickey, 2001; Mac Donnacha, Ní Chualáin, Ní Shéaghdha, & Ní Mhainín, 2005; Thomas & Williams, 2013), it is apposite to investigate the extent to which the different forms of Celtic language education align with the linguistic needs and aims of those it serves. That education makes some form of contribution to the vitality of the Celtic languages is fairly clear (McCloskey, 2001). What is less clear, however, is the exact nature of that contribution in terms of promoting positive dispositions and actual language usage outside education. A more complete picture of the role of the Celtic languages in education would emerge were the existing research augmented by studies that explore education within the broader context of the home–school–community nexus (cf. Walsh et al., 2014). Thereby, the mechanics of how exactly education, in its interaction with other factors and influences, contributes to the vibrancy of the languages might be more fully explained. Investigations are lacking of the specific pedagogical approaches that best facilitate users and learners of all proficiency levels to participate in the life of a Celtic language as appropriate to their abilities. Furthermore, additional descriptions of the sociolinguistic and pedagogical conditions that are conducive to achieving proficiency and that enable participation in the ethnoculture of habitual language users would also be welcome (e.g. Ní Chlochasaigh, 2014; chapters in Smith-Christmas, Ó Murchadha, Hornsby, & Moriarty, in press).

As education is a key focus of language policy and language planning in the Celtic languages, the factors influencing the likelihood of choice of Celtic language-medium education merit attention. Thus, the article by O'Hanlon and Patterson in this special issue focuses on the likelihood of choice of Gaelic-medium education in Scotland. The article draws on data from the 2012 Scottish Social Attitudes Survey, which includes 40 questions on Gaelic and comprises interviews with a nationally representative sample of 1229 participants over 18 years of age. Set within Baker's (2000) model of bilingual education as planning, as pedagogy and as politics, the authors use inferential quantitative methods to investigate the impact of five factors that have been found to play a role in language education in Scotland. They include demographic characteristics, exposure to Gaelic, cultural and national identities, views on the future of Gaelic and views on Gaelic in education. The authors find that while all factors contribute to the choice of Gaelic-medium education, views about the Gaelic language had the greatest impact, followed by demographic characteristics and cultural and national identity-based issues. This confirms the results from other studies on Gaelic and other Celtic languages which showed that ideological considerations rather than matters of language competence play a crucial role in the likelihood of choice of Celtic language-medium education.

Máiréad Moriarty's article in this special issue contributes further to the scholarship on the Celtic languages in education. Moriarty examines the educational potential of so-called translanguaging pedagogy in the minority language classroom. In a departure from approaches to bilingualism and second-language teaching that promote the separation of codes and the sole use of the target language, Moriarty echoes previous calls (García & Wei, 2013; Gorter, 2015) for an approach to language teaching that promotes the use of learners' previously known languages to facilitate the learning of 'new' languages. Focusing on Irish, the article advances research in translanguaging by empirically assessing the potential of this approach to minority language teaching. While the teaching of Irish has been a cornerstone of the Irish state's language maintenance policy since its foundation, it is highlighted that this approach has not, as initially hoped, resulted in high degrees of language use outside education. It is hypothesised that this is in part due to the prescribed approach to the teaching of Irish that promotes the sole use of the target language. The article uses data from a 12-week case study of integrating rap in the Irish language primary school curriculum to explore the efficacy of rap as an innovative, translanguaging resource for the teaching of Irish. The author suggests that educational resources that allow children to digress from strict normative language use and encourage the use of all social and linguistic resources for meaning making foster a more positive ideological position for Irish in the classroom and in the students' social environment. The integration of transglossic practices, it is argued, also helps to scaffold learning for different levels of competence. A further issue that consistently arises in research on sociolinguistic aspects of education in small languages concerns contention around competing linguistic norms (Ó Murchadha, 2016; Ó Murchadha, Smith-Christmas, Moriarty, & Hornsby, in press). This issue is closely related to education, but will be explored in detail in relation to the Celtic languages in the following section.

What is the target variety?

The hierarchical classification of speakers and of ways of speaking is a common social phenomenon across languages and has concerned modern sociolinguistics since its inception (Garrett, 2010). Varieties are imbued with social values and certain varieties and users are indexed as legitimate, authoritative, authentic and correct. Others do not enjoy this status. These ideological classifications are found in small languages also (Ó Murchadha et al., in press) and are attested in the Celtic varieties (Hornsby, 2005; Jones, 1998; MacCaluim, 2007; Nance, McLeod, O'Rourke, & Dunmore, 2016; Ó Murchadha, 2013, 2016; Ó Murchadha & Ó hIfearnáin, in press; Robert, 2009; Sayers, 2012). Thus, debates on target varieties for Celtic language users have been characterised by contention. The roots of contention lie in ideological assumptions about the value of traditional and post-traditional language varieties and practices and in attitudes to language users who practise those traditional and post-traditional varieties. The authority, authenticity and ownership of the languages and the ways they are practised become points of tension. This emanates from language management goals that aim to promote the use of the Celtic languages into the future. Echoing Romaine's (2006) and Bentahila and Davies' (1993) ideas, Hornsby (this issue) and Ó hIfearnáin (2015) have described how language management efforts in the Celtic languages have tended to focus on their social, cultural and linguistic *restoration* to pre-shift conditions. At the same time, the sociolinguistic *transformation* of the languages has been viewed with suspicion. Innovative linguistic features, forms and practices that have developed during shift and revival in the Celtic languages have tended to be denigrated. The post-traditional linguistic styles and practices of younger speakers and of revival or so-called 'new speakers' are strongly contested (Ó Murchadha et al., in press). Practices are denigrated that deviate from traditional forms in their phonology, grammar and syntax, in using hybrid forms that incorporate French or English, and that make more limited use of the Celtic languages in what some view as tokenistic ways. To the extent that the Celtic languages will be used into the future, however, it is likely that they will be used in an increasingly innovative fashion. In addition to documenting those practices and ideologies around them, it would be informative to illustrate the extent to which different linguistic models are successfully implemented and allow users of all levels of proficiency to participate in the lives of the Celtic languages and contribute to their vitality. Michael Hornsby's article in this special issue is a contribution to this area.

Hornsby investigates the ideological tensions that result from language shift, on the one hand, and the development of what has come to be called 'new speaker' communities for lesser used languages from the perspective of the concept of post-vernacularity, on the other. Focusing on (language) autobiographies and other narratives in the context of Breton, Hornsby explores the language ideologies of the traditional native speaker community and those of the new speakers. While both sets of speakers are very much invested in the maintenance of Breton, the two sets of speakers do not constitute a 'community', as is frequently the case, especially in the context of Celtic languages. The traditional native speaker community values Breton as a family and community language and is suspicious of the motives of the new speakers and disapproves of their language practices – both how and when they use the language – which often diverge in several ways from their own. New speakers, in contrast, are often language activists whose aim is to spread the use of the language and to increase its visibility for a variety of reasons. The activist stance is often disapproved of by the traditional speakers who actively attempt to curb these new usages among the new speakers through language policing and generally do not actively engage with new speakers.

Conclusion

Although this special issue is by no means an exhaustive account of all of the issues faced by all of the Celtic languages, it is hoped that it will advance research on sociolinguistic aspects of the Celtic languages and that it will contribute more broadly to research on the sociolinguistics of small languages and varieties. Starting from the ideological perspective that linguistic diversity is worth sustaining, we take it that a core function of the sociolinguistic enterprise in minority languages, like the Celtic languages, is to explicate the conditions and strategies that facilitate and restrict the continued use of these languages. Specifically, the articles that comprise this special issue raise important questions that are germane to issues concerning: levels of support for minoritised languages that move beyond the abstract and the symbolic; the diversification of minority language teaching methodologies to include an approach that enables all learners to engage with 'small' languages in an educational context and to contribute to the vitality of the language in a way that aligns with their own current competence; the coherence between native, traditional speakers and non-native, new speakers populations; the local language management strategies that aim to transmit the language to younger generations, but that do not necessarily conform to documented successful approaches and the social and ideological factors that influence parents' stance on minority language-medium education. Together, the articles address many of the issues that are fundamental to sustaining linguistic diversity and to the vitality of the Celtic languages.

Note

1. Although the designation 'Insular' is by now a bit of a misnomer when it comes to the Breton language, the term is used alongside the term 'Continental' in linguistic categorisations of the historical forms of the Celtic languages. Although Breton has been resident on the continent for around 1500 years, its geographical and linguistic origins are thought to lie in the insular varieties (Fife, 2009).

Acknowledgements

The writing of this article has benefitted from ongoing discussions on the themes of 'new speakers' as part of the EU COST Action IS1306 entitled, 'New Speakers in a Multilingual Europe: Opportunities and Challenges'. We would like to thank the authors, the blind reviewers and those who participated in the Celtic Sociolinguistics Symposium for their contributions in shaping this special issue.

References

Baker, C. (2000). Three perspectives on bilingual education policy in Wales: Bilingual education as language planning, as pedagogy and as politics. In R. Daugherty, R. Phillips, & G. Rees (Eds.), *Education policy making in Wales: Explorations in devolved governance* (pp. 102–123). Cardiff: University of Wales Press.

Bentahila, A., & Davies. E. (1993). Language revival: Restoration or transformation? *Journal of Multilingual and Multicultural Development, 14*(5), 355–373.

Central Statistics Office. (2012). *This is Ireland: Highlights from Census 2011 part 1.* Dublin: Stationery Office. Retrieved from http://www.cso.ie/en/media/csoie/census/documents/census2011pdr/Census_2011_Highlights_Part_1_web_72dpi.pdf

Crystal, D. (2000). *Language death.* Cambridge: Cambridge University Press.

Darmody, M., & Daly, T. (2015). *Attitudes towards the Irish language on the Island of Ireland.* Dublin: ESRI. Retrieved from http://www.gaeilge.ie/wp-content/uploads/2015/09/Attitudes-towards-Irish-2015.pdf

Davies, J. (2014). *The Welsh language: A history.* Cardiff: University of Wales Press.

Dorian, N. C. (2014). *Small-language fates and prospects: Lessons of persistence and change from endangered languages. Collected essays.* Boston: Brill.

Doyle, A. (2015). *A history of the Irish language.* Oxford: Oxford University Press.

Dunmore, S. (2014). *Bilingual life after school? Language use, ideologies and attitudes among Gaelic-medium educated adults* (Unpublished doctoral dissertation). University of Edinburgh, Edinburgh.

Economic Affairs Division Isle of Man Government Treasury. (2012). *Isle of man census report 2011.* Douglas: Isle of Man Government. Retrieved from https://www.gov.im/media/207882/census2011reportfinalresized_1_.pdf

Ferdinand, S. (2013). A brief history of the Cornish language, its revival and its current status. *e-Keltoi: Journal of Interdisciplinary Celtic Studies, 2,* 199–227. Retrieved from https://www4.uwm.edu/celtic/ekeltoi/volumes/vol2/2_6/ferdinand_2_6.pdf

Fife, J. (2009). Typological aspects of the Celtic languages. In M. J. Ball & N. Muller (Eds.), *The Celtic languages* (pp. 3–21). London: Routledge.

Fishman, J. A. (1991). *Reversing language shift: Theoretical and empirical foundations of assistance to threatened languages.* Clevedon: Multilingual Matters.

García, O., & Wei, L. (2013). *Translanguaging: Language, bilingualism and education.* Basingstoke: Palgrave Macmillan.

Garrett, P. (2010). *Attitudes to language.* Cambridge: Cambridge University Press.

George, K., & Broderick, G. (2009). The revived languages – Cornish and Manx. In M. J. Ball & N. Muller (Eds.), *The Celtic languages* (pp. 753–769). London: Routledge.

Gorter, D. (2015). Multilingual interaction and minority languages: Proficiency and language practices in education and society. *Language Teaching, 48,* 82–98.

Hickey, T. M. (2001). Mixing beginners and native speakers in minority language immersion: Who is immersing whom? *Canadian Modern Language Review, 57,* 443–474. doi:10.3138/cmlr.57.3.443

Hornberger, N. (2008). *Can schools save indigenous languages?* London: Palgrave Macmillan.

Hornsby, M. (2005). *Néo-Breton* and questions of authenticity. *Estudios de Sociolingüística, 6,* 191–218.

Jones, H. M. (2012). *A statistical overview of the Welsh language.* Cardiff: Welsh Language Board. Retrieved from http://www.poliglotti4.eu/docs/A_statistical_overview_of_the_Welsh_languagef2.pdf

Jones, M. C. (1998). *Language obsolescence and revitalisation.* Oxford: Oxford University Press.

Kavanagh, L. (2013). *A mixed methods investigation of parental involvement in Irish immersion primary education: Integrating multiple perspectives* (Unpublished doctoral dissertation). University College Dublin, Dublin. Retrieved from http://www.cogg.ie/wp-content/uploads/A-Mixed-Methods-Investigation-of-Parental-Involvement-in-Irish-Immersion-Primary-Education.pdf

MacCaluim, A. (2007). *Reversing language shift: The social identity and role of Scottish Gaelic learners.* Belfast: Cló Ollscoil na Banríona.

Mac Donnacha, S., Ní Chualáin, F., Ní Shéaghdha, A., & Ní Mhainín, T. (2005). *Staid Reatha na Scoileanna Gaeltachta.* Dublin: An Chomhairle um Oideachas Gaeltachta agus Gaelscolaíochta.

Mac-Giolla Chriost, D. (2005). *The Irish language in Ireland: From Goídel to globalisation.* London: Routledge.

Mac Gréil, M., & Rhatigan, F. (2009). *The Irish language and the Irish people.* Maynooth: Survey and Research Unit, Department of Sociology, Maynooth University.

Mas-Moury Mack, V. (2013). *Language attitudes of parents in Irish-medium primary schools in County Dublin* (Unpublished doctoral dissertation). Université Michel de Montaigne, Bordeaux &

University College Dublin, Dublin. Retrieved from https://tel.archives-ouvertes.fr/tel-01124117/document

McCloskey, J. (2001). *Voices silenced: Has Irish a future*. Dublin: Cois Life.

McLeod, W. (2014). Gaelic in contemporary Scotland: Challenges, strategies and contradictions. *Europa Ethnica*, *71*, 3–12. Retrieved from http://www.poileasaidh.celtscot.ed.ac.uk/MCLEODCATALAN2.pdf

Moseley, C. (2012). *Atlas of the world's languages in danger*. Paris: UNESCO.

Nance, C. (2015). 'New' Scottish Gaelic speakers in Glasgow: A phonetic study of language revitalisation. *Language in Society*, *44*, 553–579.

Nance, C. L., McLeod, W., O'Rourke, B., & Dunmore, S. (2016). Identity, accent aim, and motivation in second language users: New Scottish Gaelic speakers' use of phonetic variation. *Journal of Sociolinguistics*, *20*(2), 164–191.

National Records of Scotland. (2015). *Scotland's Census 2011: Gaelic report (part 1)*. Glasgow: Official Statistics. Retrieved from http://www.scotlandscensus.gov.uk/documents/analytical_reports/Report_%20part_1.pdf

Nettle, D., & Romaine, S. (2000). *Vanishing voices*. Oxford: Oxford University Press.

Ní Chlochasaigh, K. (2014). *Staidéar ar Fhoghlaimeoirí Éifeachtacha na Gaeilge ar an Dara agus ar an Tríú Leibhéal* (Unpublished doctoral dissertation). IT Tralee, Tralee.

Northern Ireland Statistics and Research Agency. (2012). *Census 2011 key statistics for Northern Ireland*. Belfast: National Statistics. Retrieved from http://www.nisra.gov.uk/Census/key_report_2011.pdf

Ó Baoill, C. (2010). *A history of Gaelic to 1800. The Edinburgh companion to the Gaelic language*. Edinburgh: Edinburgh University Press.

Ó Duibhir, P. (2009). *The spoken Irish of sixth-class pupils in Irish immersion schools* (Unpublished doctoral dissertation). University of Dublin, Dublin. Retrieved from https://www.spd.dcu.ie/site/tp/documents/Taighde_POD.pdf

Office for National Statistics. (2013). *Language in England and Wales: 2011*. London: UK Government. Retrieved from http://www.ons.gov.uk/peoplepopulationandcommunity/culturalidentity/language/articles/languageinenglandandwales/2013-03-04/pdf

Ofis Publik ar Brezhoneg. (2013). *Ar brezhoneg*. Retrieved July 7, 2013, from http://www.opab-oplb.org/54-ar-brezhoneg.htm

Ó Giollagáin, C., & Charlton, M. (2015). *Nuashonrú ar an staidéar cuimsitheach teangeolaíoch ar úsáid na Gaeilge sa Ghaeltacht* [Update of the comprehensive linguistic study of the use of Irish in the Gaeltacht]. Dublin: Údarás na Gaeltachta. Retrieved from http://www.udaras.ie/media/pdf/002910_Udaras_Nuashonr%C3%BA_FULL_report_A4_FA.pdf

O'Hanlon, F. (2015). Choice of Scottish Gaelic-medium and Welsh-medium education at the primary and secondary school stages: Parent and pupil perspectives. *International Journal of Bilingual Education and Bilingualism*, *18*, 242–259. doi:10.1080/13670050.2014.923374

Ó hIfearnáin, T. (2006). *Beartas Teanga*. Dublin: Coiscéim.

Ó hIfearnáin, T. (2015, June). *Sociolinguistic vitality after language shift and without intergenerational transmission*. Plenary paper presented at the Celtic Sociolinguistics Symposium, University College Dublin, Dublin.

Ó Murchadha, N. P. (2013). Authority and innovation in language variation: Teenagers' perceptions of variation in spoken Irish. In T. Kristiansen & S. Grondelaers (Eds.), *Language (de)standardisation in late modern Europe: Experimental studies* (pp. 71–96). Oslo: Novus.

Ó Murchadha, N. P. (2016). The efficacy of unitary and polynomic models of standardisation in minority language contexts: Ideological, pragmatic and pedagogical issues in the standardisation of Irish. *Journal of Multilingual and Multicultural Development*, *37*, 199–215. doi:10.1080/01434632.2015.1053811

Ó Murchadha, N. P., & Ó hIfearnáin, T. (in press). Converging and diverging stances on target varieties in collateral languages: The ideologies of linguistic variation in Irish and Manx Gaelic. *Journal of Multilingual and Multicultural Development*.

Ó Murchadha, N. P., Smith-Christmas, C., Moriarty, M., & Hornsby, M. (in press). *New speakers, familiar concepts?* In C. Smith-Christmas, N. P. Ó Murchadha, M. Hornsby, & M. Moriarty (Eds.), *New speakers of minority languages: Linguistic ideologies and practices*. London: Palgrave Macmillan.

SUPPORT, TRANSMISSION, EDUCATION AND TARGET VARIETIES

O'Toole, C., & Hickey, T. (2016). Bilingual language acquisition in a minority context: Using the Irish-English Communicative Development Inventory to track acquisition of an endangered language. *International Journal of Bilingual Education and Bilingualism.* doi:10.1080/13670050.2016.1179256

Price, G. (1992). The Celtic languages. In G. Price (Ed.), *Celtic connection* (pp. 1–9). Gerrards Cross: Colin Smythe.

Redknap, C. (2006). Welsh-medium and bilingual education and training: Steps towards a holistic strategy. In C. Redknap, W. Gwyn Lewis, S. R. Williams, & J. Laugharne (Eds.), *Welsh-medium and bilingual education* (pp. 1–20). Bangor: University of Wales Press.

Robert, E. (2009). Accommodating 'new' speakers? An attitudinal investigation of L2 speakers of Welsh in South-East Wales. *International Journal of the Sociology of Language, 195,* 93–116. doi:10.1515/IJSL.2009.007

Romaine, S. (2006). Planning for the survival of linguistic diversity. *Language Policy, 5,* 443–475. doi:10.1007/s10993-006-9034-3

Sayers, D. (2012). Standardising Cornish: The politics of a new minority language. *Language Problems and Language Planning, 36,* 99–119.

Smith-Christmas, C. (2014). Being socialised in language shift: The impact of extended family members on family language policy. *Journal of Multilingual and Multicultural Development, 5,* 511–526.

Smith-Christmas, C., Ó Murchadha, N. P., Hornsby, M., & Moriarty, M. (in press). *New speakers of minority languages: Linguistic ideologies and practices.* London: Palgrave Macmillan.

Statistics Canada. (2012). *Linguistic characteristics of Canadians language, 2011 census of population.* Ottawa: Statistics Canada. Retrieved from http://www12.statcan.gc.ca/census-recensement/2011/as-sa/98-314-x/98-314-x2011001-eng.pdf

Thomas, H. S., & Williams, C. (Eds.). (2013) *Parents personalities and power: Welsh-medium schools in South-East Wales.* Cardiff: University of Wales Press.

Timm, L. (2009). Language, culture and identity in Brittany: The sociolinguistics of Breton. In M. J. Ball & N. Müller (Eds.), *The Celtic languages* (pp. 712–752). London: Routledge.

Timm, L. (2013). Breton at a Crossroads: Looking back, moving forward. *e-Keltoi: Journal of Interdisciplinary Celtic Studies, 2,* 25–61. Retrieved from http://www4.uwm.edu/celtic/ekeltoi/volumes/vol2/2_2/timm_2_2.pdf

Tresidder, M. (2015). Rediscovering history and the Cornish revival. In M. C. Jones (Ed.), *Policy and planning for endangered languages* (pp. 205–221). Cambridge: Cambridge University Press.

Tristram, H. L. C. (2007). *The Celtic languages in contact.* Potsdam: Potsdam University Press.

Walsh, J., Ó Murchadha, N., Carty, N., de Bres, J., Amorrortu Gomez, E., Laugharne, J., & Nance, C. (2014). *Position paper on research themes and profiles related to new speakers of indigenous minority languages.* Retrieved from http://www.nspk.org.uk/images/WG_1.pdf

Walsh, J., & O'Rourke, B. (2014). Becoming a new speaker of Irish: Linguistic mudes throughout the life cycle. *Digithum, 16,* 67–74.

Watson, M., & MacLeod, M. (2010). *The Edinburgh companion to the Gaelic language.* Edinburgh: Edinburgh University Press.

Welsh Government, & Welsh Language Commissioner. (2015). *Welsh language use in Wales, 2013–15.* Cardiff: Welsh Government & Welsh Language Commissioner. Retrieved from http://gov.wales/docs/statistics/2016/160301-welsh-language-use-in-wales-2013-15-en.pdf

Noel P. Ó Murchadha

Bettina Migge

Celtic languages and sociolinguistics: a very brief overview of pertinent issues

John Edwards

ABSTRACT
The present and future situation of the Celtic languages is intrinsically interesting. Two are moribund, while the other four possess varying degrees of strength and institutional support. From the weakest to the strongest, however, there are pressing concerns about stability and maintenance, to say nothing of possible revitalisation. All are faced with powerful linguistic neighbours, and all have heartlands under pressure from the surrounding non-Celtic-speaking 'mainstream'. The activist community remains small and sometimes internally fragmented, and it struggles to transform a broad but passive societal goodwill – one that has, quite importantly, grown in recent years – into energised support for the language. But the Celtic languages also have a real and generalisable significance for other 'small'-language settings, inasmuch as the features that bear upon their health and development are commonly found elsewhere. This article focuses mainly upon the difficulties besetting these varieties.

Introduction

I must preface this article by noting two important limitations. First, while the Celtic-language landscape offers the same rich possibilities for sociological and sociolinguistic investigation that are available in any other linguistic environment, and while – more pointedly – language contraction and attempts at revitalisation are not the only important features of that landscape, this paper nevertheless concentrates on the long-standing and continuing aspects bearing upon maintenance, decline, and shift. For better or worse, they constitute the backdrop to much of current research and analysis. Second, it would have been impossible here to provide anything like equal or appropriately balanced time for all the Celtic languages, and so Irish and Scottish Gaelic are heavily emphasised. The effect of this limitation is, however, lessened somewhat by two factors. First, although there are size-able literatures on Breton and Welsh, they are still much less comprehensive than those for Irish and Gaelic. As for Manx and Cornish, there is very little sociology-of-language coverage indeed. Second, the social and sociolinguistic elements discussed here are relevant for vir-tually all 'small' varieties, the differences being largely ones of degree rather than of principle. Relatedly, in the presentation of a typology of minority languages, I pointed out that

SUPPORT, TRANSMISSION, EDUCATION AND TARGET VARIETIES

> while every situation is unique, the uniqueness does not arise because of elements found nowhere else – rather, it is the particular arrangement and weighting of elements that are, in fact, quite common that accounts for the unique quality of every language setting. (Edwards, 2010, p. 199)

Given cross-context similarities, it is worth mentioning that there now exists a large and burgeoning literature on 'small' and endangered languages. Up-to-date assessments include those of Austin and Sallabank (2011), Austin and McGill (2012), Sallabank (2013), and Jones (2015); see also Edwards (2009, 2010, 2015). For recent broad-brush treatments of Gaelic and Irish specifically, the reader can consult Market Research UK (2003) and Scottish Government Social Research (2011) on attitudes towards Gaelic, as well as MacCaluim (2007) and Dunmore (2014) on language use and attitudes among adult learners of the language, and those educated through the medium of Gaelic. Kennedy (2002) and Dunbar (2008) provide overviews of the vicissitudes of Gaelic language and culture in Nova Scotia. The report of the Committee on Irish Language Attitudes Research (1975) remains important, as do the more recent surveys by Mac Gréil (2009) and Darmody and Daly (2015). Other recommended overviews are found in Ó Riagáin (1997) and Mac Giolla Chríost (2005). For Irish at school, see Harris, Forde, Archer, Nic Fhearaile, and O'Gorman (2006) and the very recent report by Smyth and Darmody (2016); see also the relevant chapter in Darmody and Daly (2015).[1] Chapters devoted to Gaelic in both Scotland and Nova Scotia, and to Irish, may be found in Edwards (2010); see also Edwards (in press-a).

A summary of almost a dozen of the important issues and difficulties relating to the maintenance of the Celtic languages can be found in Edwards (1985), and a slightly altered categorisation appeared in Edwards (2010). Either version can be easily consulted. I prescind, then, from further general treatment here, and – with regard to the languages that I am *not* focusing on – will only touch upon one or two pieces of work; these have been chosen not only for their recency and cogency, but also because of the generalisable points that they emphasise. I should also point out again that – in *all* the discussion that follows – I am particularly concerned with problems, with matters that hamper the maintenance and growth of the Celtic languages. I am not unaware, of course, of the positive developments of recent years, of the continuing work of scholar-activists, of the community interest that has increased in some parts of the *Gaeltacht* and the *Gàidhealtachd*, and of the language provisions made in the media, in arts and culture forums, in the linguistic landscape – and of course in schools. But any rational survey of the contemporary scene will immediately highlight the fragility of many language settings, the uncertainty about reliable and ongoing support (financial and otherwise – and the latter is what essentially underpins the former), the lack of continuity when so much is asked of so few activists, and other related difficulties. Many linguistic endeavours of the past, the present, and no doubt the future reveal the operation of what, in a quite different context, Dr Johnson (no friend to the Highlands and Islands one might think, if a little mistakenly) referred to as the triumph of hope over experience.

Breton, Welsh, Manx, and Cornish

Recent work by Ó hIfearnáin (2013) and Hornsby (2015) suggests continuing difficulties for Breton. There is, for instance, persistent reliance on educational programmes to stem decline and to effect growth. This has always been a misguided, if understandable, emphasis; for the most recent of my criticisms here, see Edwards (2012). Beyond the general mistake of placing too many eggs in the school basket, there are practical and immediate problems. One of these has to do with teacher availability, in part because of limited competence among relatively small numbers of interested teachers, and in part because of limited state support for training and positions. Student (i.e. parent) demand is not always what revivalists hope for, and teacher limitations often mean that even those who are interested in learning in or about the language may not find room in classroom programmes. This in turn suggests an unfavourable circle. As well, in Ó hIfearnáin's (2013, p. 133) discussion of the *Ya d'ar brezhoneg* ('Yes to Breton') campaign that is underwritten by the Office of the Breton Language, we read about the 'small number of professionals … charged with enormous responsibility for language promotion' and about 'enthusiasts', the 'core group of language activists' who began, and continue, to animate the movement.[2] Breton, he adds, now has some considerable general support (it is 'currently fashionable in many circles'), more perhaps among younger people than among the older generation of actual speakers, who often failed to transmit the language to their children. Such support, we know, typically remains at a rather passive level of goodwill; it also seems to exemplify Hansen's (1952) famous notion of the third-generation 'return' of interest in ethnicity, language, and other manifestations of 'groupness'.[3]

Evans (2015), a scholar at the Cardiff office of the Wales Institute of Social & Economic Research (Data and Methods), reports that, while they acknowledged the importance of Welsh, fewer than half of a large sample of young teenagers indicated that they would speak it as adults. The census results of 2011 suggested a substantial growth in the number of Welsh speakers over the preceding decade, but more recent figures show that – as a proportion of the overall population – the number of those able to speak Welsh has declined. Evans thus describes the hopes following the establishment of the Welsh Assembly (in 1998) as part of a 'false dawn' for the language. (It should, of course, be remembered that Welsh still remains in a better position than either Irish or Scottish Gaelic.[4]) Evans concludes with observations that are now very familiar across a wide range of 'small' languages: transmission to, and use by, the younger generation is faltering; general views of the language are favourable – but essentially passive; and active intervention on the part of both governmental and non-governmental agencies is of limited use in the face of the overall linguistic tenor of ordinary life.

Writing about Manx, Ó hIfearnáin (2015) suggests that 'vitality' remains largely among what is a tiny 'core group' of revivalists. Sallabank (2013, p. 9) adds that 'campaigners for the Manx language … trace continuity via linguists and enthusiasts who learned the language from traditional native speakers in the 1950s, to a new language community of highly proficient adult speakers'. This core, then, has at least some connection to a language spoken within recent memory; Ned Maddrell, allegedly the last native speaker of Manx, died in 1974, and there are recordings of his speech (and that of a few others). Such a connection, however slender, is not available for Cornish. Price (1984, p. 134) rather harshly wrote that 'I shall reserve the term [Cornish] for genuine Cornish and shall refer to pseudo-Cornish as "Cornic"', adding that 'Cornic is not Cornish … "revived" Cornish is not real Cornish. It could perhaps be compared to a painting so heavily restored as no longer to qualify as an authentic work by the [original] artist' (p. 144). In short, he said, any Cornish revival effort is 'a highly artificial exercise' (p. 71). As may be imagined, the argument is a heavily debated one in revivalist circles, and it has been raised in many contexts beyond the Celtic ones. Sallabank (2013), again, is worth consulting on Manx, and we can also note that – *pace* Price – initiatives continue to arise. One of the latest is reported by Eichler (2015): undertakings by the Cornwall Council (motto: *Onen hag Oll* – that is, 'One and All'), the county authority, to maintain some bilingual signage, and to provide 'language awareness training' to council staff. The latter would seem to mean, essentially, teaching employees to say a few Cornish words of greeting.

Gaelic

Having already indicated that this paper was not meant to cover familiar ground, I restrict myself here to very recent reports on one or two themes of intrinsic and generalisable interest – essentially education, culture, and the media. Furthermore, in an attempt to stray somewhat beyond the usual academic precincts, I provide here some relevant information gleaned from the last two years of the *West Highland Free Press*. For more than four decades, this weekly has focused upon 'land and language' in the region, and, since it has a broadly pro-Gaelic stance, one can be reasonably sure that criticisms concerning the maintenance and development of the language are not based upon linguistic antipathy.

If we turn first to educational matters, we find a letter-writer lamenting the lack of qualified teachers of Gaelic (MacPherson, 2014). In the same issue, an editorial commented on the 'long search for a permanent head teacher at the Gaelic school in Inverness' (Anon, 2014a, p. 27).[5] Seven months later, another editorial (Anon, 2015a, p. 2) reported that such a teacher had finally been appointed, also noting that two earlier head teachers had not been Gaelic speakers. In the next issue, under a headline reading 'One school's gain is another school's loss' (Anon, 2015b, p. 15), we learn that the new head teacher for *Bun-sgoil Ghaidhlig Inbhir Nis* had been 'poached' from her former school in Broadford. Falconer (2015) reported that the *Fàs Mòr* nursery school in Sleat (on Skye) would close unless appropriate childcare staff could be found. Also in Sleat, MacKenzie (2015a, p. 3) wrote that *Bun-sgoil Shlèite* is about to lose a Gaelic teacher, because pupil numbers for the coming term 'will be four short of what is required to justify the third teacher'. (The overall number of children in Gaelic-medium classes there would be 44.) Some 700 parents and others then called for the local authority to review the decision to cut a teaching position, and the authority agreed to discuss the matter further (Anon, 2015d, p. 3). In fact, however, as Macdonell (2015) reported several days later, the cut went ahead, leaving only two Gaelic teachers. A thoughtful article (MacLeod, 2015a) put the teacher problem into a little wider perspective; among other things, the author noted that, in 1980, Boyd Robertson – then the vice-president of *An Comunn Gàidhealach*, and now the principal of *Sabhal Mòr Ostaig* – was critical of the lack of provision of Gaelic teachers. The problem is thus hardly a new one. A related point was raised by Galbraith (2015, p. 15) in favour of Gaelic at school; she nevertheless wrote that some 'pro-language legislation may actually encourage hostility towards the language'. 'Councils need to want to provide Gaelic-medium education', she observed, 'not merely feel coerced into it'.

Discussion of Gaelic in the media has also taken up a great deal of newspaper space, and the predominant topic is the operation and the programming of *BBC Alba*, established as a Gaelic-language television channel in 2008, and on the air for about seven hours a day. One report (Anon, 2014b) criticised the use of spoken English and English subtitles; the fear is that *BBC Alba* may become a much more general – and generally anglophone – 'Scottish' channel. The criticism was echoed in a balanced letter from MacNeacail (2015a) – as well as in less temperate contributions from Dòmhnullach (2015, p. 15), who wrote that 'the idea that this is a channel for the Gaelic language and culture is not credible', and from Scholes (2015, p. 17): 'what we have is a hybrid, dumbed-down, pandering-to-the-masses, English-language-dominant travesty, which tries to serve everyone but ends up serving no-one'. One outcome was an 'open letter' to *BBC Alba*, in which Bowie (2015, p. 15) and 14 others called for a 'substantial increase in the actual use of Gaelic … to provide Gaelic speakers with the television service they deserve'.[6] A little later, Hamish Fraser, speaking at the Oban *Mòd* as chair of the Highland Council's Gaelic Implementation Group, called for more Gaelic on television; more specifically, he argued that 'BBC Alba should have the same broadcasting hours as S4C [*Sianel Pedwar Cymru*, i.e. Channel Four Wales] in Wales' (Anon, 2015e, p. 19; see also the interesting 'opinion' piece by Aonghas Caimbeul, 2015). A note by Dòmhnall Caimbeul (2015a), the Chief Executive of *MG Alba* (the Gaelic Media Service – a government body which partners with the BBC to produce Gaelic-language programming) then suggested that parity with Welsh-language programming was indeed being requested in the renewal of the charter on which all BBC broadcasting is based. We next heard from MacDonald (2015, p. 13), arguing that *BBC Alba* now has 70% English content, and suggesting that the channel 'is continuing to reinforce public exhibition of the Gaels' inferiority complex'; see also MacNeacail (2015b). The reply this elicited from Caimbeul (2015b) was a four-paragraph example of non-informative bureaucratese.

Beyond television provision for Gaelic, or the lack thereof, there has been much recent discussion about official support, or the lack thereof, for artistic and cultural activities and events. MacKenzie (2015b, p. 1) reported that 'Creative Scotland, the public agency for Scottish arts', has rejected three applications for funding from organisers of the 2015 *Mòd* in Oban. He quoted John Morrison, the chief executive of *An Comunn Gàidhealach*, as saying that 'they [Creative Scotland] fail our Gaelic community, the Gaelic traditional arts community, and the Gaelic creative community'. Without making specific reference to the *Mòd*, a spokesperson for Creative Scotland pointed to the support that it does provide for other Gaelic bodies and events (Anon, 2015f). The main leader in that week's number of the *West Highland Free Press* agreed with Morrison, however (Anon, 2015g). Giving the Sabhal Mòr Ostaig lecture a fortnight later, Nicola Sturgeon – the leader of the Scottish National Party (SNP) and First Minister – announced some very modest funding (to be divided, however, among some 40 different groups) in support of Gaelic initiatives in 'early years' organisations (Anon, 2015h). MacLeod (2015b, 2015c) described the lack of support from *Bòrd na Gàidhlig* that has led to the termination of *Pròiseact nan Ealan*, the national Gaelic arts agency. Its chief executive spoke of a 'disillusioned' arts sector. As is typical in cases like this, interpretations vary and emotions run high, but we can at least agree with MacLeod (2015c, p. 14) when he wrote that 'all is not well in the small world of Gaelic development … *Bòrd na Gàidhlig* itself [is] in something of a state of crisis'.

Irish

The treatment here centres upon some limited – but important – reappraisals of earlier work. As with the preceding discussions, the intent is to highlight continuing themes of relevance and, again, work presented in a non-academic medium – if the *Times Literary Supplement* can be so called – is touched upon here.

The report of the Committee on Irish Language Attitudes Research (1975) presented the findings of the first large-scale survey of its kind, and it remains one of the most comprehensive assessments of Irish (although not without faults: see below). The following is an extract:

> The average individual ... feels rather strongly that the Irish language is necessary to our ethnic and cultural integrity, and supports the efforts to ensure the transmission of the language. At the same time, under present policies and progress, he is not really convinced that we can ensure its transmission ... has a rather low or 'lukewarm' *personal* commitment to its use ... strongly supports nearly all government efforts to help the Gaeltacht, but at the same time feels that the language is not very suitable for modern life. (Committee on Irish Language Attitudes Research, 1975, p. 24 – my italics)

'Many people', the report continued, 'would characterise these conflicting beliefs and feelings about the language as rather "schizophrenic" ... [but] it will, we hope, become clearer how people can hold these apparently contradictory beliefs' (p. 24).

In 1977 I wrote a review of the Committee's report. In it, I suggested that Irish had become for most a symbolic, cultural quantity; that there was scant sense of any future growth in vernacular Irish use; and that people were coming to understand that relying upon the schools as the main revival agents was a mistake. I also suggested that – technically and methodologically sophisticated as the Committee's work had been – its lengthy report (almost 500 pages) lacked clear and substantial summaries. One consequence was that it seemed possible for quite different points of view to find support for their arguments: 'shortly after the report was made public, both the Gaelic League ... and the Language Freedom Movement [broadly opposed to revival efforts] ... welcomed it as vindicating their positions' (Edwards, 1977, p. 58). While suggesting that its findings illuminated 'the central issues, policy options and potentials' and while hoping that 'an improved basis for future language planning' had been established, the report acknowledged that 'it was not our function to say what future policies ... ought to be' (Committee on Irish Language Attitudes Research, 1975, p. 364). A few months before the official release of the report, Fishman (1975) – one of the three overseas members of the 16-person Committee – stated that, having provided little interpretation of the *meaning* of the information presented, the report remained rather inconclusive. Kiberd cited some of what I have extracted here from the report, and went on to note that, while published in 1975, the words 'still hold true' (1995, p. 570).

Confirmation of Kiberd's observation may be found in more recent work, including that of Darmody and Daly (2015), who – in pointing out that attitudes and usage reflect the influence of education, the family, and the 'wider community' – are essentially covering every single base! One should cite, as well, Mac Gréil's (2009) large-scale survey of Irish abilities, attitudes, and use. It reveals, above all, the same favourable but largely passive attitudes towards Irish held by most; it also makes what history would suggest are unreasonable demands on the education system. Unlike the 1975 survey, however, this report does not shy away from recommendations, and its closing pages are full of 'shoulds'. So, for example, Mac Gréil (p. 121) tells his readers that the transmission and promotion of competence in 'living Irish' should be a pedagogical priority; that all relevant agencies should agree on a new 'strategic plan'; that all signs, notices, and retail labels should be in both Irish and English; and that all public announcements should be bilingual. This is the usual rounding up of the usual suspects.

The report is also interesting because its author, like other language activists, is sometimes prone to exaggeration, something that is worth mentioning here as a generalisable cautionary note.[7] Mac Gréil decided, for instance, 'to take "occasionally or more often" as the cut-off point' for categorising informants as 'regular users' of Irish (p. 114) – who then comprise about 23% of Irish-born respondents. Similarly, something like 47% are reported as 'reasonably competent' in the language. He also notes, incidentally, a recent 'growing interest in learning Irish in the United States and Canada' (p. 118) – a point which, if at all true in terms of tiny numbers, is trivial, a point of essential misinformation.[8] A foreword by Maolsheachlainn Ó Caollaí – a former President of *Conradh na Gaeilge* – adds to the curious combination of generality plus unreality that Mac Gréil provides. Ó Caollaí suggests that it was only the report of the Committee on Irish Language Attitudes Research (1975) that revealed the influence of 'social language norms on the speaking of Irish' (p. x) (he means here that only when potential interlocutors are competent in, and willing to use, the language will it actually occur in conversation, which is hardly earth-shaking). He then adds that the lack of general use of vernacular Irish is not because – as he suggests some 'opponents' have claimed – people have rejected the language but, rather, because 'the existence and influence of the [social language] norms has [sic] never been explained to the public, and no effort made to change them' (p. xi).

Two particularly rich commentaries are found in a recent number of the *Times Literary Supplement* (5 June 2015). The first is Declan Kiberd's joint review of a history of the important Irish-language publishing house, Sáirséal agus Dill, and of an English translation of what is probably its most famous book.[9] The second is a review, by Jon Day, of three new books about Brian O'Nolan (Brian Ó Nualláin), who wrote as both Flann O'Brien and Myles na gCopaleen.[10] Both essays deal with the Irish scene, of course, and each reminds us of matters that remain important – not only in that particular setting but, indeed, also in others where 'smaller' and 'larger' languages come into contact. Some brief attention to them, then, is very much to my purpose here.

The Irish-language publishing house Sáirséal agus Dill was established in 1947. Two years later, it brought out Máirtín Ó Cadhain's *Cré na Cille* – an Irish classic. The title of the book, which Kiberd (2015, p. 7) refers to as 'the greatest novel in the language', has usually been given in English as *Graveyard Clay*, but it has just appeared in an English translation, by Alan Titley, as *The Dirty Dust* (2015). Ó Cadhain 'once told his students in Trinity College that, but for Seán Ó hÉigeartaigh [the publisher], he would have lost the will to write' (Kiberd, 2015, p. 7). This would be high praise for any publisher, but here it has a special significance, both in the particular context of an emerging modern Irish literature, and the more general social setting of the language itself. Here is Kiberd's characterisation of the latter:

> A state founded in 1922 had, by its standardizing of Gaeltacht idiom and pursuit of moral rectitude in texts, wrung much of the life out of a language which it claimed to revere … the texts studied in Irish classes reflected a narrow nationalist ideology … by the 1940s much of the early fire had gone out of the language revival movement. A free state invented by artists and intellectuals had become a tedious theocratic bureaucracy. (p. 7)

Kiberd went on to suggest that Ó Cadhain's graveyard setting may have:

> reflected his despair about the very idea of language revival, the argument in the 1940s being less about how to save Irish than about exactly who had responsibility for disposing of the embarrassingly vociferous corpse. The setting may have a further meaning. The author was looking to a future when his book, like certain Latin classics, would live on after its own language had fallen out of daily use. (p. 8)

Finally, Kiberd noted that, 'despite Ó Cadhain's fears, it [Irish] still survives, albeit precariously, as a community language' (p. 8).

In the second *Times Literary Supplement* review, Day (2015) argued for the importance of Brian O'Nolan: 'an immensely gifted writer in Irish – perhaps, alongside Máirtín Ó Cadhain, the greatest of the twentieth century' (p. 10). A native Irish speaker, O'Nolan (as Myles na gCopaleen) wrote the popular 'Cruiskeen Lawn' column in the *Irish Times* from 1940 until 1966, as well as *An Béal Bocht*, a novel published in 1941 and subsequently translated into English (as *The Poor Mouth*) in 1973.[11] The book's subtitle is *A Bad Story About the Hard Life* (*An Milleánach, Droch-Sgéal ar an Droch-Saoghal* – a reproach, a bad story about the hard life). In his preface, Patrick Power – O'Nolan's translator – wrote that it 'should have acted as a cauterisation of the wounds inflicted on Gaelic Ireland by its official friends' (O'Nolan, 1973, p. 6).[12] In a later English version of the book, the cover blurb notes that this 'scathing satire on the Irish ... brought down on the author's head the full wrath of those who saw themselves as the custodians of Irish language and tradition' (O'Brien, 1996). These are the *Gaeilgeoirí*, often referred to by O'Nolan as 'the Gaeligores' – literally, 'Irish speakers' but generally with the connotation of narrow and blinkered enthusiasm. O'Nolan's commitment to the language itself was powerful, and it was this intensity of feeling that led him to be so critical. 'The present extremity of the Irish language', he wrote, 'is due mainly to the fact that the Gaels deliberately flung that instrument of beauty and precision from them' (see Ó Conaire, 1973, p. 125). Contemporary historians and sociologists of language would not characterise the decline of Irish in such a way, of course, but the strength of feeling is the point here.

In more disinterested quarters, in fact, *An Béal Bocht* 'was a very great success ... well received by the critics and hailed as a "classic of writing in Irish"' (Clissmann, 1975, p. 238). Indeed, O'Nolan's work was praised by writers as varied as Sean O'Casey, William Trevor, John Updike, S. J. Perelman, Anthony Burgess, and James Joyce; some of their laudatory comments can be found prefacing O'Brien (2000). Then as now, the feeling – at least outside the narrowest of Irish circles – was that the novel was at once a comic masterpiece, a powerful satire, and a lament for that disappearing 'instrument of beauty'.

Day acknowledged that the 'political dimensions' of O'Nolan's work have come in for renewed attention, but continued by suggesting that his writing in Irish 'remains lamentably under-explored' (p. 10). To some extent at least, the second phrase weakens the first, since the original version of *An Béal Bocht* was a powerful satire, Swiftian in its sweeping attack on what Day himself referred to as the 'navel-gazing gloom of the Gaeltacht' (p. 10). Murphy (2014, p. 143) cited O'Nolan's own assessment of his book – 'a parody' and 'a prolonged sneer' at Tomás Ó Criomhthain's (1929) 'misery memoir': his famous autobiographical account of life in the Blaskets, *An t-Oileánach* (*The Islandman*).[13] This is a bit unfair to both books, particularly since O'Nolan (as Kiberd, 1995 and other scholars have pointed out) had real admiration for Ó Criomhthain's book.[14] (He was not,

SUPPORT, TRANSMISSION, EDUCATION AND TARGET VARIETIES

however, an admirer of Robin Flower's 1934 English translation.) Nonetheless, he was very critical of narratives that described extreme poverty, extolled it as ennobling and 'authentic' – and then saw in that 'authenticity' the one true heartland of the Gael and the Irish language. Day thus commented on the 'fetishization of poverty that [O'Nolan] associated with the Irish literary revival' and went on to cite the criticism made by the author himself (in one of his newspaper pieces) of revival figures like Synge, Yeats, and Lady Gregory, who 'persisted in the belief that poverty and savage existence on remote rocks was [sic] a most poetical way for people to be, provided they were other people' (p. 10).[15]

I have written elsewhere about the ill-judged – if convenient – romanticism which has animated language revivalists in many 'small'-language settings; see, for instance, Edwards (2011; in press-b). Kiberd (1995, p. 498) wrote of 'the Dublin revivalists … who could idealize the saintly simplicity of western life, only by ignoring the awful poverty on which it was based'.[16] The linking of geographical remoteness, poverty, and 'poetry' (this last term now more usually glossed as 'authenticity') is certainly a powerful one, and for several reasons. First, physical distance implies a removal from the urban gaze of intellectuals, a gap that allows attractive imagery to be maintained in unsullied fashion. Any actual contact with the far-flung corners where the true Gaels (for example) live need not tarnish cherished images, because it is typically fleeting and often selective. At the height of the Irish revival effort, the famous but narrow-minded Trinity College professor, John Mahaffy (1899) – who criticised the 'Celtic craze' and the potential for an unfavourable recrudescence of Irish speaking – did acknowledge that some competence in Irish might be useful 'to a man fishing for salmon or shooting grouse in the West' (Gaelic League, 1901, p. 2). Second, the poor have often been described as having a sort of innate morality or, indeed, nobility. Nature and/or nurture may have provided only meagre resources, but simplicity and lack of affectation are among the virtues of the unsophisticated peasant life. Caution is advised here, of course. 'The superior virtue of the oppressed' was the ironic title Bertrand Russell gave to one of his 'unpopular essays', a title reflecting the curious 'admiration for groups to which the admirer does not belong' (1950, p. 80). Here we find reference to the 'simple annals of the poor', and the long-standing romanticising of the 'noble savage' – a figure now resuscitated, Russell tells us, in the form of 'the patriot of an oppressed nation'.[17] The point has been enlarged by Pirie (1985, p. 109): 'the poor may indeed be blessed, but they are not necessarily right. It is a fallacy to suppose that because someone is poor they must be sounder or more virtuous than one who is rich' – this, as Pirie notes, is a version of the *argumentum ad Lazarum*. The romanticisation and moral ennobling of the poor are easily countered, of course, by dispassionate and intelligent observation, but it is interesting that such a perspective has been specifically and linguistically highlighted. Ó Danachair (1969, p. 120) wrote of the association of Irish in the Gaeltacht with 'penury, drudgery and backwardness' – words almost identical to those used by Dunn (1953, p. 134), who referred to 'the incessant toil, hardship, and scarcity peculiar to primitive conditions' which led to the association of Gaelic in Nova Scotia with 'poverty and ignorance'.

Discussion

This treatment, as implied at the outset, is both brief and selective. The issues raised, however, are familiar ones, and so brevity and selectivity need not mean loss of generalisability. Here are the main points that highlight ongoing concerns for the Celtic languages. The first is simply the fragility of any language community that has shrunk substantially in the face of a powerful neighbour, particularly when (as in the cases under specific discussion here) that neighbour is not only of immediate or local importance, but is also of broad and increasing global scope. Second, one notes the continuing reliance upon educational intervention on behalf of language maintenance; while understandable, the fact that it is sometimes justified on the grounds that the same system which once neglected the language can now resuscitate it reveals a poor grasp of social evolution and change. A corollary here has to do with the perennial shortage of competent and committed teachers; this adds practical difficulties to the more theoretical one just mentioned. Another point is that efforts on behalf of 'at-risk' varieties are typically made by a small 'core' group of activists; the weakness of such efforts is obvious, particularly when those committed to the language – scholars, teachers, language learners, community organisers, and so on – are not native speakers. It is striking how many language revivalists have either come from elsewhere, physically or linguistically, or are – often through higher education, travel, etc. – rather atypical group members. Of course, leaders *are* often atypical in one way or another, but the point remains important, particularly when one factors in the 'fashionability' that language efforts can sometimes possess. It cannot be assumed, after all, that such attractiveness will be a constant.

One also notes a thread of broad but passive goodwill that is evident in so many settings. To galvanise this, to turn what has sometimes become largely symbolic into something more immediately communicative, is always a challenge. And when maintenance or revival efforts are made, the question of exactly *what* is to be rejuvenated may come to the fore. One need not think of such an extreme case as the 'Cornic' so disdained by Professor Price, but only of other instances within the Celtic world of the problems associated with dialect choice, or suitable 'mixing' among dialects when some sort of standard is aspired to, or even of the fact that a revived medium may not fully please any segment of the language community. Further, are revival efforts themselves so limited, either by social circumstance or by restricted intent or aspiration, that their most common outcome is some thin and generally unused linguistic wash, or the *cúpla focal* uttered or written as a small cultural offering – an offering which in some eyes may be seen as a mark of goodwill, but in others as tokenism?

The problems associated with 'small'-language media are also common, as is the continuing difficulty of securing and maintaining support for cultural and artistic manifestations. There is genuine dismay that small amounts of uncertain funding are provided to help in what is already a fragile situation. This regret is surely heightened in circumstances in which public pronouncements, official acknowledgement, bilingual signage, and the like are revealed as little more than facile lip service. The uncertainty or apparent insincerity of support is, of course, a reflection of the low level of public – of *active public* – concern with the language. It may in fact be taken as a rough marker of the degree to which broad but passive favourability is translated into something more tangible.

I should finally say something about the appearance and the impact of O'Nolan-like parody. It is, as I hope to have shown, nothing like a simple or crude rejection of language-maintenance efforts. On the contrary, it stems from a deep concern for the language, coupled with deep disappointment about the unrealistic and counterproductive excesses of 'enthusiasts', about the unhealthy and inaccurate romanticisation of regions from which many inhabitants have long wanted to leave, about the idealisation of unsophisticated 'authenticity' and peasant down-to-earthiness which is maintained by regarding them from a useful distance, and about the dangerous association which is seen to inevitably connect vernacular continuity with penury and hardship.

I present this litany of difficulty on the basis of a stance which is critical but not hostile – a difference which not everyone, within and without the academic community, has always been ready or willing to accept. I believe, however, that no disinterested concern for the fortunes of the Celtic varieties can neglect what are the real and powerful hindrances to maintenance and revival. I will not repeat here the criticisms I raised elsewhere (see Edwards, 2012, for instance), but the actual historical record of maintenance efforts is open to all who would see. Putting aside questions of linguistic and cultural morality – if such an animal can be appropriately or usefully described – recognition of what seems to be reality is the essential first step in coming to grips with the relationships in which 'larger' and 'smaller' languages are entwined. But what then follows? Cultural continuity can certainly be maintained after vernacular shift, archival work and record-keeping have never been better technically enabled, and even the educational provisions that I have described here as very limited agents of revival can, after all, at least open doors for those who wish to persevere. As well, Nancy Dorian (1987) pointed out that even maintenance efforts that fall short may have value in increasing cultural awareness, in acting as spurs or foundations for future work, and so on.

Revivalists hope for much more, of course – and in all cases (even with Manx and Cornish, perhaps) there still exist language communities; sometimes, indeed, these remain sizeable, even if very small in terms of overall populations. The single most important action is to galvanise these communities in more effective ways, to create more activists from the ground up, as it were. This is of course easy and perhaps glib to say. But there seems little doubt that engaged and ongoing grass-roots activity is the key – now more possible than ever, with at least the superficial and often shallow acceptance of diversity shown by the larger linguistic community. Support from outside, of course, has been and will continue to be welcome. As D.P. Moran once remarked, however, in his commentary on the Irish revival (1900, p. 268): 'without scholars [revival] cannot succeed; with scholars as leaders it is bound to fail'.

In a pair of recent articles, Ó Giollagáin (2014a, 2014b) has provided an interesting analysis of the history and contemporary status of Irish-language policy.[18] He argued that, by the 1970s, the government had essentially abandoned any meaningful pro-Irish policy. He then suggested that there was a continuation of what is but a 'superficial aura' of support, even in the *Gaeltacht*. Official and semi-official language agencies there may be, but they are not generously underpinned, nor is there any deep or sincere wish for this 'sub-contracting' of the language effort (particularly where language learning is involved) to thrive. One thinks of some biblical washing of the hands. In his recent conference presentation, Ó Giollagáin (2015) advocated rejecting such 'language policy', abandoning utopian or 'aspirational' thinking, and accepting what he feels to be the real situation – and his sense of what is real coincides pretty well with the picture I have sketched in this article. I believe this to be an accurate and generalisable picture. I also agree with his suggestion that future initiatives should emanate from renewed and strengthened grass-roots organisation. Again, all this is easy to say, and rather short on specifics. But if the picture were clearer, and the way ahead more obvious, much of the literature on 'small' and threatened languages would be of only historical interest.

Conclusion

At the heart of all the problems and obstacles outlined here is the blunt fact that vernacular language shift is a symptom of broader social contact or, indeed, conflict. It follows that attending to language in isolation is like treating measles by covering up the spots. It also follows that attempting to go beyond what is symptomatic involves much deeper social change, and this is something that is generally of very limited appeal. To change metaphors, what is typically wanted is a sort of selective reweaving of the social fabric, in which alterations in language use leave untouched desirable social evolutions. If we were satisfied with better recording and documentation of threatened or endangered languages, then the tools at our disposal and the opportunities for traditional linguistic description and analysis were never better. If we are not, if we hope for 'ordinary' or vernacular language maintenance, then the task is much more daunting.

The general sociolinguistic and sociology-of-language literature bearing upon 'small' or 'at-risk' varieties, as exemplified in the several examples cited in the introduction, is now both broad and deep. Edited collections, important monographs, and a large number of chapters and articles are easily available, and even the most cursory inspection will reveal many cross-context similarities. As I noted earlier, every setting is unique, but its singularity does not come about through the presence of elements found nowhere else. The uniqueness occurs, rather, through the particular arrangement and weighting of regularly recurring features. And one finds that the Celtic-language issues discussed here are particularly instructive.

Notable, of course, is the weakness of endangered varieties. While there commonly exists a broadly favourable set of attitudes towards 'small' languages, these rarely lead to effective and enduring social action. Only among core groups of activists is goodwill energised. We have also seen here a reliance upon the educational system to effect language change. This is understandable, but insufficient, and often places unwarranted and unwanted burdens upon teachers. These are the most important generalities that link Celtic languages to others. It is also appropriate to mention here one or two other features whose presence so far has been only implicit.

Not even the most committed of language activists contemplate a return to monolingualism in endangered varieties. What is envisaged is a durable bilingualism or diglossia, in which domains – I have elsewhere been more specific, referring to 'domains of necessity' (Edwards, 2010) – continue to exist for the language in question. Predation and the gradual invasion of domains are a feature, however, of language-contact landscapes involving stronger and weaker varieties. A related point has to do with the nature of bilingualism itself. In an increasing number of contexts, we see a growth in 'secondary' bilingualism coinciding with an ongoing decrease in the 'primary' variety. The former refers to the competence gained, usually in fairly self-conscious and formal ways, by adults; while this can occur for obvious material reasons, it often reflects a language-and-identity commitment. The latter, on the other hand, typically marks earlier and less formal acquisition. To put it crudely, bilingualism via instruction versus bilingualism learned 'naturally', or, in some circumstances at least, the addition of a new language to a long-existing monolingual base versus native or near-native dual competence. It is not difficult to see that bilingualism in its 'primary' format is likely to have a deeper cultural significance than its counterpart. There is, of course, absolutely nothing wrong with learning a new language as an adult but, when bearing in mind that cultural significance, that affective link between language and an identity which is seen to be somehow less 'authentic' in the absence of the original variety, it is easy to see that – for example – the growth of bilingualism in urban centres, and in purpose-built educational facilities, has rather less lustre than a linguistically healthy heartland.

It is possible, as I have mentioned, to accuse some language activists of an overly enthusiastic and unrealistic romanticism, a posture that might be seen to map onto the bilingual distinction I have just drawn. That is, the linguistic nationalism of those animated by a Yeatsian 'passionate intensity' is rarely found in the surviving *Gaeltachtaí* of the world. It is, of course, to be expected that activists, some of them linguistic converts who did not learn the threatened language at their mother's knee, will serve as leaders. That is what activists do, or try to do. Those whose linguistic capabilities they hope to champion are – while hardly to be described as 'lacking all conviction' – not usually in the forefront of change. Indeed, in the deepest and the most 'authentic' heartlands we find, to cite Marx (1852/1981, p. 124), people who 'cannot represent themselves; they must be represented'. A century later, Gellner (1964, p. 162) made a similar observation: 'the self-image of nationalism involves the stress on folk, folklore, popular culture [and we could of course highlight the ancestral language here] … genuine peasants or tribesmen … do not generally make good nationalists'. Citing 'peasants and tribesmen' may not strike quite the appropriate note here, but if we bear in mind the frequent revivalist use of words like 'genuine' and 'authentic' to describe linguistically beleaguered populations, then the sense remains. The role of leaders is obvious and necessary, but the difficulty of the task increases when they are unlike their 'followers' in important cultural ways. Where leaders *are* 'of the people', where they too are (for example) 'primary' bilinguals, they are still often separated by education, inclination, and residence.

Most of the 'small'-language communities of the world that have any sense of decline and shift, and any wish to attempt countermeasures, now have more means and may benefit from more general public awareness than at any time in the past. They must also contend, however, with ever more intrusive linguistic neighbours. In this situation, it is common to see greater animation among activists coupled with an increasing degree of preaching to the converted. Thus, the tone of language reports and surveys is often quite hortatory, more prescriptive than one now expects to find in social-scientific analyses, more heavily loaded with words like 'should' and 'ought' – and, not unrelatedly, prone to exaggeration. An example already cited here is the work of Mac Gréil (2009). Another is a 2004 report by the (Nova Scotian) Gaelic Development Steering Group; here we find mention of a 'long-range strategy … a twenty-year vision … five-year action plans … a mission statement' (p. 9) and, overall, statements that are enthusiastic but naive. The only results that can be guaranteed to flow from such reports are more reports. In a useful historical and contemporary overview of Gaelic in Nova Scotia, Kennedy (2002, p. 114) commented on a conference in which 'stakeholders' employed a 'consensus-building approach' to issue a report about future options for Gaelic development, a report that 'unfortunately … did not appear to result in any concrete action'. Just so.

SUPPORT, TRANSMISSION, EDUCATION AND TARGET VARIETIES

In this article, I have sketched out what, in the main, are depressing facts for those interested in the current and future status of 'small' languages and, more specifically, for those concerned with language revitalisation. It is surely important, however, to face such facts; indeed, ignoring them is not an option for the disinterested scholar. I would be the last person to deny that progress of a sort has been made in some limited quarters, and I reiterate here my personal preference for a vibrant and enduring multilingual landscape. But it is necessary, surely, to attempt some balance when so much of the literature – for Celtic varieties and many others – encourages unrealistic expectations. Hope is important, but so is experience.

Notes

1. The brief report of Smyth and Darmody (2016) is not always crystal clear. Noting that children tend to see Irish as a less interesting and more difficult subject than English and mathematics, the authors go on to add that 'those whose families speak Irish at home are much less likely to find Irish not interesting, but surprisingly this group of young people does not display a higher level of interest in Irish' (p. 6). Towards the end of the paper, they write: 'as can be expected, and echoing findings from the adult population (see Darmody and Daly, 2015), students whose families speak Irish at home are least likely to dislike Irish. Interestingly, however, they are not necessarily more likely to have more positive dispositions towards the subject' (p. 14). Perhaps we are meant to understand that children from Irish-speaking families like the language, but do not necessarily find it an interesting school subject.
2. Ó hIfearnáin uses the word 'enthusiasts' here, but the term does not suit everybody. Some see in it a lowering of the status of language scholar-activists. Others apply it to 'non-scholars' – those whose fervour outstrips their capacity for rational analysis.
   At the 2015 UCD symposium on Celtic Sociolinguistics, Wilson McLeod essentially endorsed Ó hIfearnáin's interpretation. And, he added, is not everyone who studies anything an enthusiast? So why only use the term in language contexts where the subtext is rather derogatory? An interesting point, to which I shall return (but not here!).
3. 'Hansen's Law' states that 'what the son wishes to forget the grandson wishes to remember' – the implication being that it is only when immigrant groups become reasonably well established that they have the time to consider matters of heritage. It is not difficult to see how this 'law' could be extended to other situations involving linguistic and cultural shift. See Hansen (1938, 1952).
4. Recent census figures suggest that about 20% of the Welsh and Breton populations speak the language, with about half that percentage being fluent; the latter figure drops to about 3% for Irish and even less for Scottish Gaelic. These are, of course, very rough categories, and there is a large literature on the interpretation of census figures, on the ways in which questions are asked, on definitions of language ability and use, and so on. Maté's chronological overview (1997) of the Celtic languages remains useful (and is cited by Darmody & Daly, 2015). For general observations on census interpretation, see Edwards (1995).
5. Interim staffing problems seem general, and not confined to education: one reads that, in mid-2015, even *Bòrd na Gàidhlig* itself had to appoint a non-Gaelic-speaking chief executive (Anon., 2015c).
6. It is perhaps worth mentioning that two of the 15 signatories were Robert Phillipson and Tove Skutnabb-Kangas, well-known scholar-activists. It seems that only three or four of the Scottish signatories have academic affiliations, although these are not mentioned. None of the more familiar Scottish language scholars affixed their names (or perhaps they were not asked to).
7. While the tone of many of his statements makes it apparent that Mac Gréil is far from being a dispassionate observer, one can also read on the website advertisement of his autobiography (2014) a description of him as a 'lifelong Irish language promoter'. In the report (2009, p. 117),

SUPPORT, TRANSMISSION, EDUCATION AND TARGET VARIETIES

he writes that 'the results were disappointing in that the majority of the people did not see the true basis of Irish ethnic identity, i.e., the Irish language'.

8. I must also point out here another factor which weighs on the value of Mac Gréil's presentation – the bizarre, selective, and inadequate embedding of the work in what is now a large and nuanced literature. Apart from reference to the work of the Committee on Irish Language Attitudes Research (1975), there are no bibliographical entries at all to work in the sociology or the sociolinguistics of Irish (or any other language). There *are*, however, references made to Emory Bogardus's work in the 1920s and 1930s on social distance, to Robert Merton's social theory, and to a 1938 report on the famous 'Hawthorne' (observer) effect.

9. The two books reviewed by Kiberd are Ó hÉigeartaigh and Nic Gearailt (2014) and Ó Cadhain (2015).

10. The books reviewed by Day are Murphet, McDonald, and Morrell (2014), Borg, Fagan, and Huber (2014), and Long (2014).

11. *The Poor Mouth* is subtitled *A Bad Story about the Hard Life*, and shown as being 'edited' by Myles na Gopaleen (Flann O'Brien) – this revealing a slightly anglicised version of the surname, as well as yet another of Brian O'Nolan's (or, indeed, Brian Ó Nualláin's) pseudonyms.

    'Cruiskeen lawn' is *crúiscín lán*, a small full jug, and 'Myles na gCopaleen' is 'Myles of the little horses (or ponies)'. Both are terms that O'Nolan took from *The Colleen Bawn* (*cailín bán*, beautiful girl), a popular play written by Dion Boucicault in 1860. In the play, Myles is a lovable rascal, who at one point praises the familiar small but brimming jug. An example of the title character in another of Boucicault's plays – *The Shaughraun* (1874) – he is a man who is 'the soul of every fair, the life of every funeral, the first fiddle at all weddings and patterns' ('shaughraun' = *seachránaí*, a vagabond, a rover).

12. The translator, Patrick C. Power, is not an earlier scholar of that same name and middle initial – an historian, archaeologist, academician, and Canon of the church – but a more contemporary Gaelic scholar and teacher.

13. Ó Criomhthain is not the only author whose work is satirised by O'Nolan: 'many critics have pointed to the novel's parodic relationship with the works of Séamus Ó Grianna, Muiris Ó Súilleabháin, Peig Sayers, Peadar Ó Laoghaire [and] Tomás Ó Máille' (Murphy, 2014, p. 143).

14. Beyond his discussion of O'Nolan, Kiberd also makes room in his lengthy study (1995) for the critical views of Brendan Behan, Patrick Kavanagh, and others who were particularly angered by the actions and the pretensions of 'the nationalists'.

15. The 'other people' are often characterised as sublimely unique. In his English translation of *An t-Oileánach* (Ó Criomhthain, 1929), Robin Flower gives the author's original *mar ná beidh ár leithéidí arís ann* as 'because our likes will not be there again' (p. 323), and this rather immodest statement – the sort of attribution best made by others – provided much fodder for O'Nolan. In Power's translation of *An Béal Bocht*, this line appears in the first paragraph of the first chapter: 'our types will never be there again, nor any other life in Ireland comparable to ours who exists no longer' (p. 11). And the very last lines of book are these: 'Certainly, I suffered Gaelic hardship throughout my life – distress, need, ill-treatment, adversity, calamity, foul play, misery, famine and ill-luck. I do not think that my like will ever be there again' (p. 125). Between the start and the end of the book, the 'likes' who or which will never recur refer to the immediate neighbours (p. 13), the house in which the author was born (p. 21), Ambrose the pig (p. 28), the Gaelic-speaking inhabitants of Corkadoragha (p. 42), the Gaeligores (p. 49), festival participants (p. 61) – and even the weather on Hunger-Stack Mountain: 'it was an amazing place and very amazing also was the weather. I think its like will not be there again' (p. 105).

    I also cannot resist here providing an excerpt in which O'Nolan satirises the visiting 'Gaeligores'. One of them, the President of the Corkadoragha *feis*, in fact, is made to say (pp. 54–55):

> Gaels! … it delights my Gaelic heart to be here today speaking Gaelic with you at this Gaelic feis in the centre of the Gaeltacht … I myself have spoken not a word except Gaelic since the day I was born … and every sentence I've ever uttered has been on the subject of Gaelic … He who speaks Gaelic but fails to discuss the language question

SUPPORT, TRANSMISSION, EDUCATION AND TARGET VARIETIES

is not truly Gaelic in his heart … There is nothing in this life so nice and so Gaelic as truly true Gaelic Gaels who speak in true Gaelic Gaelic about the truly Gaelic language.

16. Kiberd (1995, p. 501) also reminds us that, while the inhabitants of Corkadoragha disdain traditional names (like Seán and Séamas), the 'affluent Gaelic revivalists from Dublin … are equally anxious to conceal their own inherited names'. One immediately thinks, with Kiberd, of Douglas Hyde, whose pseudonym *An Craoibhín Aoibhinn* ('the pleasant little branch') deflects attention from a surname that 'pointed back to invading English soldiery'.

17. Russell mentioned the 'annals of the poor' without attribution, no doubt feeling that his readers would need none. It is taken from Thomas Gray's *Elegy Written in a Country Churchyard* (1751) – where the poet observes that the annals of the poor are not only simple, but also short. This is, of course, reminiscent of what Thomas Hobbes (1651) had to say exactly 100 years earlier, in the thirteenth chapter of *Leviathan*: without civil government, human life is generally 'solitary, poor, nasty, brutish and short'.

18. For the comprehensive and data-rich work underpinning Ó Giollagáin's assessment of Irish in the *Gaeltacht*, see Ó Giollagáin and Charlton (2015): this is the updated version of a report initially published in 2007.

Disclosure statement

No potential conflict of interest was reported by the author.

References

Anon. (2014a, October 17). *Another interim head for Gaelic school*. West Highland Free Press, p. 27.

Anon. (2014b, December 12). *Gaelic TV channel criticised for English content and subtitles*. West Highland Free Press, p. 10.

Anon. (2015a, May 8). *New head is appointed for Gaelic school in inverness*. West Highland Free Press, p. 2.

Anon. (2015b, May 15). *One school's gain is another school's loss*. West Highland Free Press, p. 15.

Anon. (2015c, July 17). *Gaelic agency defend non-Gael's appointment*. West Highland Free Press, p. 2.

Anon. (2015d, August 21). *Council to consider case for maintaining teacher numbers*. West Highland Free Press, p. 3.

Anon. (2015e, October 16). *Fraser calls for more Gaelic on television*. West Highland Free Press, p. 19.

Anon. (2015f, October 9). *Creative Scotland hit back at claims of Gaelic exclusion*. West Highland Free Press, p. 3.

Anon. (2015g, October 9). *John Morrison is right – Creative Scotland is failing the Gaelic community*. West Highland Free Press, p. 15.

Anon. (2015h, October 23). *First Minister delivers Sabhal Mòr lecture*. West Highland Free Press, p. 1.

Austin, P., & McGill, S. (Eds.). (2012). *Endangered languages*. London: Routledge.

Austin, P., & Sallabank, J. (Eds.). (2011). *The Cambridge handbook of endangered languages*. Cambridge: Cambridge University Press.

Borg, R., Fagan, P., & Huber, W. (Eds.). (2014). *Flann O'Brien: Contesting legacies*. Cork: Cork University Press.

Bowie, G. (2015, April 24). *An open letter to BBC Alba*. West Highland Free Press, p. 15.

Caimbeul, A. (2015, October 23). *Beachd*. West Highland Free Press, p. 12.

Caimbeul, D. (2015a, October 16). *How renewed BBC charter can best serve Gaelic*. West Highland Free Press, p. 13.

Caimbeul, D. (2015b, November 6). *Gaelic media 'best agent' for revitalisation of language*. West Highland Free Press, p. 15.

Clissmann, A. (1975). *Flann O'Brien: A critical introduction to his writings*. Dublin: Gill & Macmillan.

Committee on Irish Language Attitudes Research. (1975). *Report*. Dublin: Government Stationery Office.

SUPPORT, TRANSMISSION, EDUCATION AND TARGET VARIETIES

Darmody, M., & Daly, T. (2015). *Attitudes towards the Irish language on the island of Ireland*. Dublin: Economic and Social Research Institute.

Day, J. (2015, June 5). *Corduroys vs the tyro*. Times Literary Supplement, pp. 9–10.

Dòmhnullach, A. (2015, January 30). *'Embarrassed' by much of what Gaelic TV has to offer*. West Highland Free Press, p. 15.

Dorian, N. (1987). The value of language-maintenance efforts which are unlikely to succeed. *International Journal of the Sociology of Language, 68*, 57–67.

Dunbar, R. (2008). *Minority language renewal: Gaelic in Nova Scotia, and lessons from abroad*. Halifax: Department of Communities, Culture and Heritage (Gaelic Affairs Division).

Dunmore, S. (2014). *Bilingual life after school? Language use, ideologies and attitudes among Gaelic-medium-educated adults* (PhD thesis). University of Edinburgh.

Dunn, C. (1953). *Highland settler: A portrait of the Scottish Gael in Nova Scotia*. Toronto: University of Toronto Press.

Edwards, J. (1977). Review of Report (Committee on Irish language attitudes research). *Language Problems and Language Planning, 1*, 54–59.

Edwards, J. (1985). *Language, society and identity*. Oxford: Blackwell.

Edwards, J. (1995). *Multilingualism*. London: Penguin.

Edwards, J. (2009). *Language and identity*. Cambridge: Cambridge University Press.

Edwards, J. (2010). *Minority languages and group identity: Cases and categories*. Amsterdam: John Benjamins.

Edwards, J. (2011). *Challenges in the social life of language*. Basingstoke: Palgrave Macmillan.

Edwards, J. (2012). Review of Can schools save indigenous languages? (N. Hornberger, Ed.). *Language Policy, 11*, 201–203.

Edwards, J. (2015). Endangered languages: A survey of surveys. *Journal of Multilingual and Multicultural Development, 36*, 444–450.

Edwards, J. (in press-a). Minority languages and group identity: Scottish Gaelic in the old world and the new. In S. Preece (Ed.), *The Routledge handbook of language and identity*. London: Routledge.

Edwards, J. (in press-b). Language rights … and wrongs. In Y. Peled, & D. Weinstock (Eds.), *The ethics of language*. Oxford: Oxford University Press.

Eichler, W. (2015). *Council approves new Cornish language plan*. http://www.localgov.co.uk/Council-approves-new-Cornish-language-plan/39774

Evans, D. (2015). *Language apathy for speaking Welsh reveals struggle to keep it as a living language*. http://theconversation.com/teenage-apathy-for-speaking-welsh-reveals-struggle-to-keep-it-as-a-living-language/48422

Falconer, L. (2015, July 10). *Gaelic nursery in Sleat faces closure due to staff shortages*. West Highland Free Press, p. 2.

Fishman, J. (1975, August 15). *Interview*. Irish Times.

Gaelic Development Steering Group. (2004). *Developing and preserving Gaelic in Nova Scotia: Strategy for a community-based initiative*. Halifax: Department of Tourism, Culture and Heritage.

Gaelic League. (1901). *The Irish language and Irish intermediate education II: Evidence of Dr Mahaffy … .* Dublin: Gaelic League.

Galbraith, M. (2015, July 3). *Elements of Gaelic-medium education proposals 'smack of compulsion'*. West Highland Free Press, p. 15.

Gellner, E. (1964). *Thought and change*. London: Weidenfeld & Nicolson.

Gray, T. (1751). *An elegy wrote in a country church yard*. London: Dodsley & Cooper.

Hansen, M. (1938). *The problem of the third generation immigrant*. Rock Island, IL: Augustana Historical Society.

Hansen, M. (1952). The third generation in America. *Commentary, 14*, 492–500.

Harris, J., Forde, P., Archer, P., Nic Fhearaile, S., & O'Gorman, M. (2006). *Irish in primary schools: Long-term national trends in achievement*. Dublin: Department of Education and Science.

Hobbes, T. (1651). *Leviathan, or, the matter, forme, & power of a common-wealth ecclesiasticall and civill*. London: Crooke.

Hornsby, M. (2015). *Revitalizing minority languages: New Speakers of Breton, Yiddish and Lemko*. Basingstoke: Palgrave Macmillan.

Jones, M. (2015). *Policy and planning for endangered languages*. Cambridge: Cambridge University Press.

Kennedy, M. (2002). *Gaelic Nova Scotia: An economic, cultural and social impact study*. Halifax: Nova Scotia Museum (Department of Tourism and Culture).

Kiberd, D. (1995). Flann O'Brien, Myles, and *The Poor Mouth*. In *Inventing Ireland: The literature of the modern nation* (pp. 497–512). London: Cape.

Kiberd, D. (2015, June 5). *A talking corpse*. Times Literary Supplement, pp. 7–8.

Long, M. (2014). *Assembling Flann O'Brien*. London: Bloomsbury.

MacCaluim, A. (2007). *Reversing language shift: The social identity and role of Scottish Gaelic learners*. Belfast: Cló Ollscoil na Banríona.

MacDonald, A. (2015, October 30). *BBC Alba reinforces the inferiority complex of the Gaels*. West Highland Free Press, p. 13.

Macdonell, H. (2015). *Seven hundred sign petition as Skye school drops Gaelic teacher*. http://www.thetimes.co.uk/tto/news/uk/scotland/article4537332.ece

Mac Giolla Chríost, D. (2005). *The Irish language in Ireland: From Goídel to globalisation*. London: Routledge.

Mac Gréil, M. (2009). *The Irish language and the Irish people*. Maynooth: Department of Sociology (Survey and Research Unit).

Mac Gréil, M. (2014). *The ongoing present*. Dublin: Messenger.

MacKenzie, K. (2015a, July 3). *Sleat parents call for Gaelic teaching post to be restored*. West Highland Free Press, p. 3.

MacKenzie, K. (2015b, October 9). *Arts agency snub Mòd and spark 'favouritism' row*. West Highland Free Press, p. 1.

MacLeod, M. (2015a, October 23). *Still not enough Gaelic-medium teachers to meet the needs*. West Highland Free Press, p. 14.

MacLeod, M. (2015b, November 27). *Gaelic arts agency no longer able to go on*. West Highland Free Press, p. 2.

MacLeod, M. (2015c, November, 27). *Pròiseact closure sparks fears for future of Gaelic arts*. West Highland Free Press, p. 14.

MacNeacail, A. (2015a, February 27). *BBC Alba output 'just not very Gaelic'*. West Highland Free Press, p. 3.

MacNeacail, A. (2015b, November 13). *UK and Scottish government must act to support Gaelic language*. West Highland Free Press, p. 13.

MacPherson, A. (2014, October, 17). *Gaelic expansion hampered by lack of teachers*. West Highland Free Press, p. 13.

Mahaffy, J. (1899). The recent fuss about the Irish language. *Nineteenth Century, 46*, 213–222.

Market Research UK. (2003). *Attitudes to the Gaelic language*. Glasgow: MRUK.

Marx, K. (1852/1981). *The eighteenth Brumaire of Louis Bonaparte*. New York, NY: International.

Maté, I. (1997). Changes in the Celtic-language-speaking populations of Ireland, the Isle of Man, Northern Ireland, Scotland and Wales from 1891 to 1991. *Journal of Multilingual and Multicultural Development, 18*, 316–330.

Moran, D. (1900). The Gaelic revival. *New Ireland Review, 12*, 257–272.

Murphet, J., McDonald, R., & Morrell, S. (Eds.). (2014). *Flann O'Brien and modernism*. London: Bloomsbury.

Murphy, N. (2014). Myles na gCopaleen, Flann O'Brien and *An Béal Bocht*: Intertextuality and aesthetic play. In R. Borg, P. Fagan, & W. Huber (Eds.), *Flann O'Brien: Contesting legacies* (pp. 143–155). Cork: Cork University Press.

O'Brien, F. (1996). *The poor mouth*. Normal, IL: Dalkey Archive Press.

O'Brien, F. (2000). *Further cuttings from 'Cruiskeen Lawn'*. Normal, IL: Dalkey Archive Press.

Ó Cadhain, M. (1949). *Cré na cille*. Dublin: Sáirséal agus Dill.

Ó Cadhain, M. (2015). *The dirty dust*. (A. Titley, Trans.). New Haven: Yale University Press.

Ó Conaire, B. (1973). Flann O'Brien, *An béal bocht*, and other Irish matters. *Irish University Review, 3*, 121–140.

Ó Criomhthain, T. (1929). *An t-Oileánach*. Dublin: Clólucht an Talbóidigh.

SUPPORT, TRANSMISSION, EDUCATION AND TARGET VARIETIES

Ó Criomhthain, T. (1934). *The Islandman*. (R. Flower, Trans.). London: Chatto & Windus.

Ó Danachair, C. (1969). The Gaeltacht. In Brian Ó Cuiv (Eds.), *A view of the Irish language* (pp. 112–121). Dublin: Government Stationery Office.

Ó Giollagáin, C. (2014a). Unfirm ground: A reassessment of language policy in Ireland since independence. *Language Problems and Language Planning, 38*, 19–41.

Ó Giollagáin, C. (2014b). From revivalist to undertaker: New developments in official policies and attitudes to Ireland's 'first language'. *Language Problems and Language Planning, 38*, 101–127.

Ó Giollagáin, C. (2015). *Post-language planning: A new deal for Gaelic identity in Ireland*. Paper to the Celtic Sociolinguistics Symposium, University College Dublin, 25 June.

Ó Giollagáin, C., & Charlton, M. (2015). *Nuashonrú ar an staidéar cuimsitheach teangeolaíoch ar úsáid na Gaeilge sa Ghaeltacht: 2006–2011*. Galway: Údarás na Gaeltachta.

Ó hÉigeartaigh, C., & Nic Gearailt, A. (2014). *Sáirséal agus Dill, 1947–1981: Scéal foilsitheora*. Dublin: Cló Iar-Chonnacht.

Ó hIfearnáin, T. (2013). Institutional Breton language policy after language shift. *International Journal of the Sociology of Language, 223*, 117–135.

Ó hIfearnáin, T. (2015). Sociolinguistic vitality of Manx after extreme language shift: authenticity without traditional native speakers. *International Journal of the Sociology of Language, 231*, 45–62.

O'Nolan, B. (1941). *An béal bocht*. Dublin: Preas Náisiúnta.

O'Nolan, B. (Myles na gCopaleen). (1973). *The poor mouth*. (P. Power, Trans). London: Hart-Davis MacGibbon.

Ó Riagáin, P. (1997). *Language policy and social reproduction: Ireland, 1893–1993*. Oxford: Clarendon.

Pirie, M. (1985). *The book of the fallacy*. London: Routledge & Kegan Paul.

Price, G. (1984). *The languages of Britain*. London: Edward Arnold.

Russell, B. (1950). *Unpopular essays*. London: George Allen & Unwin.

Sallabank, J. (2013). *Attitudes to endangered languages: Identities and policies*. Cambridge: Cambridge University Press.

Scholes, D. (2015, February 20). *Gaelic speakers deserve 'proper' TV channel*. West Highland Free Press, p. 17.

Scottish Government Social Research. (2011). *Attitudes towards the Gaelic language*. Edinburgh: Scottish Government.

Smyth, E., & Darmody, M. (2016) *Attitudes to Irish as a school subject among 13-year-olds* (Working Paper no. 525). Dublin: Economic and Social Research Institute.

'Is it really for talking?'[1]: the implications of associating a minority language with the school

Cassie Smith-Christmas

ABSTRACT
This paper examines how caregivers in a bilingual family discursively link Gaelic to a school context when interacting with Maggie, an eight year-old who is currently enrolled in Gaelic Medium Education on the Isle of Skye, Scotland. The paper argues that the caregivers achieve this discursive framing primarily through treating Gaelic as a performance language and through orienting to discourses that de-normatise Maggie's use of her minority language. The paper argues that although the caregivers believe they are *encouraging* Maggie's use of Gaelic, by framing the language in a school context, they link Gaelic to authority. It is further argued that this association of Gaelic with authority may be one of the many contributing factors to Maggie's low use of the language overall. The paper concludes by discussing the implications of this argument in terms of language policy and planning.

Introduction

Immersion language education can play a vital role in revitalising an autochthonous minority language. In areas where the language shift is so acute that the language is no longer used as a regular mode of communication in the family and/or community, for example, the school can be one of the primary sites children are able to acquire the language fluently (see for example, Baker, 2007; King, 2000; Ó Baoill, 2007). However, despite this potential role in what Fishman (1991) refers to as 'Reversing Language Shift' ('RLS') and the existence of minority language education at Stage 4 of Fishman's well-known Graded Intergenerational Disruption Scale, Fishman also warns (1991, 2001) against using education as a convenient solution to the intricate problems that arise when a language recedes from everyday life. Spolsky (1991) takes a similar stance to Fishman, arguing that the real challenge in education as an RLS strategy lies in ensuring that pupils use the language *outside* the classroom. This difficulty is not one which is necessarily easily surmountable, as illustrated by Fishman's (1996, p. 79) recounting of his friend John MacNamara's experience as a student in an Irish immersion school:

> He [John Macnamara] was scolded one day by the lady who ran a candy store. He had just bought the candy from her and began talking English to his sister. 'You have learned Irish all your life. How come you're speaking English? You should be talking Irish to your little

sister.' Later, out on the street, the sister asked him, 'Is Irish really for talking?' That really did happen. It had not occurred to them that Irish was for talking. It was a school subject like geography and arithmetic.

The revelation that minority language immersion education does not necessarily result in pupils' use of the language *outside* the classroom is well-documented in the case of the Celtic languages, which serve as the focus of this special issue (for examples, of this premise in other linguistic contexts, see Hornberger, 2008; Woolard, 2011). Research in Wales (e.g. Edwards & Newcombe, 2005), Ireland (e.g. Harris, 2005) Brittany (e.g. Ó hlfearnáin, 2011), the Isle of Man (e.g. Clague, 2009) and Scotland (e.g. O'Hanlon, McLeod, & Paterson, 2010; Will, 2012) shows that while pupils may have the ability to speak the respective Celtic language due mainly or in part to the role of the school, social use of the language remains limited. The dominant language persists on the playground, a reality which, as demonstrated in Hodges' work in Wales (2009) and Dunmore's work in Scotland (2015), often carries forth into these pupils' adult lives. There are a number of reasons for the lack of social use of the minority language, but underpinning them all are the realities of language shift and the reflexive relationship between these realities at the macro and the micro level; as Harris (2005, p. 974) writes in the case of Irish, pupils 'know that there are very few occasions outside (particularly involving their peers) in which there might be either a real need, or even an opportunity, to speak it'. The need for complementary efforts in language planning, particularly those which link the home domain to the school, have been recognised (e.g. Armstrong, 2014; Edwards & Newcombe, 2005; Smith-Christmas & Armstrong, 2014) and programmes such as *Twf* in Wales have sought to build such bridges; however, the challenge of expanding the use of the minority language beyond the classroom remains a formidable one.

The purpose of this paper is to demonstrate how a child (Maggie, aged eight and four months at the time of the recording), as well as various adults in her family (Maggie's great-aunt Isabel and aunt Màiri), seem to view their minority language – Scottish Gaelic – in the same light as John MacNamara's sister. Given the apparent ubiquity of classroom minority language use not translating to social minority language use, this is perhaps not surprising; however, what is surprising is that not only does Maggie come from a home where a number of her family members harbour very pro-Gaelic ideologies and enact these ideologies in everyday language practices (in other words, the school and the home complement one another in terms of Maggie's minority language experience), but that this view is *strengthened* by the Gaelic-speaking adults' actions within this particular conversational episode. Through microinteractional analyses of selected excerpts from a recorded interaction, this paper will explore how although the adults appear to think they are *encouraging* Maggie to use Gaelic, in reality, the way in which they frame Gaelic reifies English as the language for, as John MacNamara's sister puts it, 'talking' and equates Gaelic with didacticism. The paper explores the ideological underpinnings of this framing, postulating that they might in part be a facet of the blame-shifting that sometimes accompanies language shift (cf. Kroskrity, 2009), thus providing further insight into often self-perpetuating nature of language shift and adding further perspective to the challenges of using education as a tactic for minority language revitalisation.

Scottish Gaelic in education

Scottish Gaelic, henceforth referred to simply as 'Gaelic', is an autochthonous minority language spoken by fewer than 58,000 speakers in Scotland (National Records of Scotland, 2013). The 1872 Education Act, which for the first time made education compulsory in Scotland between the ages of 5 and 13, made no mention of Gaelic and not only was Gaelic excluded from the curriculum, but pupils were reportedly beaten for using their native language in school (see, for example, MacKinnon, 1974, p. 55). It was not until more than century later that Gaelic education provision came to fruition with the introduction of the Bilingual Education Project in the mid-1970s (see MacLeod, 2003; McLeod, 2003; Robertson, 2003). This was followed by the introduction of Gaelic immersion early years playgroups and in 1985, Gaelic immersion education extended to the primary level, with the first two Gaelic Medium Education (GME) units established in Glasgow and Inverness, the total number of students of which was 24 (O'Hanlon, 2010). Throughout the years, GME has grown considerably; in 2011–2012, there were 2418 pupils at primary level receiving their tuition through the medium of Gaelic (0.7% of the total primary roll), while 1104 pupils at secondary level were being taught through the medium of Gaelic (0.4% of the total secondary roll) (Galloway, 2012). On the Isle of Skye, which serves as the locus of this particular study (and where according to the most recent census, 29.4% of the population speaks Gaelic), there are currently 91 nursery pupils and 244 primary pupils enrolled in GME; a further 121 secondary pupils are taking subjects taught through the medium of Gaelic (Highland Council website, 2015; see also Müller, 2006 for more on secondary GME provision in Skye).

However, despite these growing numbers, and despite pupils' attainment in terms of linguistic competence in Gaelic, English is the peer group language of GME children and remains so when they grow older, thus diminishing its potential as an effective RLS strategy (see Dunmore, in press). One of the reasons for this widespread language practice is that with the exception of three schools located in urban areas, all GME schools are 'units' within wider English-medium schools, meaning that English is the language of communal school spaces and the wider pupil population (see Armstrong, 2013; Morrison, 2006). However, being part of a Gaelic-only school does not necessarily mean that students use Gaelic outside the classroom (see Nance, 2013); as detailed in O'Hanlon et al. (2010, p. 44), a high proportion of children in GME are from homes where Gaelic is not used and/or from areas where community use of Gaelic is low or non-existent and thus are more comfortable using English. As Will (2012), however, shows in her study of GME pupils on the Isle of Lewis, even pupils from strongly Gaelic-speaking families and areas tend to use English outside the classroom. One of Will's explanations for this is that within the bounds of classroom, Gaelic is reified as the compliance code and in contrast, the use of English elicits 'opportunities for rebellion' (p. 119), functioning as a way for pupils to distinguish their personal identities from their school identities.

Will's hypothesis became instrumental in formulating my own argument (see Smith-Christmas, 2016) that the association of Gaelic with authority is another reason why, in addition to the shift-perpetuating realities already in place in a family on Skye referred to as the 'Campbell family',[2] the youngest members of this family developed an early and continuing preference for English. In one interaction (p. 102), for example, eight year-old Maggie states that she uses English on her 'free breaks' and also that she does not use Gaelic at home because she is 'not in school'. This last statement not only lends support to Will's suggestion that English may function as a way for GME children to distinguish their personal identities from their school identities, but also suggests that Maggie strongly associates Gaelic with school. As school is the most authoritative domain within Maggie's sociocultural landscape, I further contend that this association leads to a link between Gaelic and authority, which is compounded by other realities within Maggie's family as well as her wider community (cf. Meek, 2007). The aim of this paper therefore is to lend credence to these assertions by embarking on an exploration of the interaction from which Maggie's 'free breaks' and 'cause I'm not in school' declarations are drawn. In doing so, I will examine the ways in which two caregivers (Isabel, Maggie's great-aunt, and Màiri, Maggie's aunt) discursively strengthen the association between Gaelic and school and thereby with authority. I will demonstrate that while the caregivers' motivations *appear* to lie in a desire for Maggie to use more Gaelic, the framing of these requests and comments works against this goal and further contributes to perpetuating language shift in the family. The paper will conclude by postulating the possible motivations for Isabel and Màiri's particular framings and will situate these motivations within the ideological landscape of language revitalisation in Scotland.

Method

This article is situated in an eight-year ethnography of the Campbell family. The particular excerpts analysed in this paper are drawn from an interaction recorded on the last night of a series of recordings (approximately six hours) of the family's naturally occurring conversations in the home environment in July 2014. The aim of this corpus was to replicate as closely as possible a similar corpus of the family's interactions in July 2009, on which I based my Ph.D. thesis. Speakers were aware that they were being recorded and signed consent forms prior to recording both corpora. The fact that I was constantly recording and had a close relationship with the family meant that for the most part, the effects of the Observer's Paradox were mitigated.

However, occasionally my presence *did* seem to have an effect on speakers' language use and while these interactions may not be *completely* representative of the family's everyday language use, they are extremely valuable in discovering how certain latent ideologies come to the forefront of family consciousness (see also Smith-Christmas, 2014). The interaction under scope in this paper is one such example and I contend that in this interaction, my presence was largely responsible for the admonishing stances that the caregivers take towards Maggie in critiquing her lack of Gaelic use. In this particular interaction, Maggie, Nana (Maggie's paternal grandmother), Isabel (Nana's sister and Maggie's great-aunt), Màiri (Nana's daughter and Maggie's aunt) and I are finishing a Chinese takeaway meal and waiting for Maggie's mother and siblings to arrive at the house so that we can have a *cèilidh* – that is, a party where the children perform what they have learned at the *Fèis*, a summer programme in which children take traditional music, dance and sports classes through the medium of Gaelic. It should be emphasised here that although

Màiri and Isabel may come across as slightly harsh in these excerpts, their utterances, especially Màiri's, were said in a light-hearted manner. As is consistent with my other work on the Campbell family, I use a microinteractional approach (cf. Auer 1984) in analysing these conversations. Transcription conventions are given at the end of this article.

Gaelic as a performance language

Before moving on to the core of the analysis, it is necessary to outline some pertinent background information about the four key speakers in this interaction. Nana, who was in her late 60s at the time of the recording, is very overt in her pro-Gaelic ideologies and along with the children's mother, Nana is one of the main actors in setting up the Gaelic-centred Family Language Policy (see Smith-Christmas, 2014, 2016). In contrast to Nana, Nana's sister Isabel frequently uses English with both adult interlocutors as well as Nana's grandchildren; in fact, Isabel's total monolingual Gaelic use in the 2014 Corpus totalled only 20% of her total conversational turns[3] (see Smith-Christmas, 2016). Isabel is nine years younger than Nana and this age difference is hypothesised to account in part for Isabel's relatively low use of Gaelic. Similar to Isabel, Nana's daughter Màiri, who was raised by Nana as a Gaelic speaker, generally uses English with other interlocutors and reserves the use of Gaelic for occasional talk directed to the third generation.

Thus, it is clear to see that among the adult speakers, Gaelic is not a normative and habitual practice for all speakers in the family. This reality, along with the other language shift-inducing practices present in the family and the wider community, all contribute to the third generation's low use of Gaelic (see Smith-Christmas, 2016 for much further detail). Thus, from an early age (3;4 in the 2009 Corpus), it was clear that Nana's granddaughter Maggie had developed a strong preference for English. This reality has not changed in the five years since the 2009 Corpus; in the 2014 Corpus, for example, only 5% of Maggie's total conversational turns were coded as 'Monolingual Gaelic'.[4] Explaining all the various contributing factors to Maggie's low use of Gaelic is far beyond the scope of this article, so I have chosen to focus on one aspect in particular: the occasional didactic framing of Gaelic and how this ultimately serves to position the use of Gaelic as an aberrant language choice (i.e. non-normative) in family interactions. Given that the Campbell family as a whole are *trying* to maintain the language with the third generation, this positioning seems counterproductive and the goal of this particular analysis is not only to examine this positioning in terms of its potential effect on Maggie's overall use of Gaelic, but also to shed light on the possible origin of this positioning and what this can tell us about the reflexive nature of language shift and revitalisation.

The following two sections therefore analyse the mechanisms by which the caregivers enact this particular discursive positioning. One of the ways in which it is achieved appears to be through framing Gaelic as an *object* to be *performed*, not as an everyday normative mode of communication. The first instance of this framing occurs when I ask Maggie in Gaelic how many students there are in her classes at the *Fèis* and she begins counting to herself in English. Isabel then asks Maggie if she can count in Gaelic and Maggie rises to Isabel's challenge, as seen below:

SUPPORT, TRANSMISSION, EDUCATION AND TARGET VARIETIES

Excerpt 1

1	Isabel	*an urrainn dhut cunntadh anns a' Ghàidhlig?*
		can you count in Gaelic
2	Maggie	yuh huh (0.9) >*aon dhà trì*
		one two three?
		[intervening numbers in Gaelic]
		trichead 's a naoi /forty @@@
		thirty-nine
3	Nana	@@
4	R	@@
5	Maggie	@@ forty one forty two forty three
		ceithread 's a::: ceithir
		forty-four
		[intervening numbers in Gaelic] /fifty @@@ fifty one fifty two fifty three fifty [[four fifty five fifty six @@@]
6	Isabel	[[fifty *ceithir* fifty *còig* fifty *sia* fifty *seachd*]
		four five six seven
7	Maggie	fifty seven- fifty *seachd* fifty [[*ochd*]
		seven eight
8	Isabel	[[fifty *ochd*]
		eight
9	Maggie	fifty *naoi*:::(1.4) [[fifty (eleven)]
		nine
10	Isabel	[[*tri fichead*]
		sixty
11	R	@
12	Maggie	@@
13	Isabel	(fifty)
14	Maggie	I don't think I can say any more
15	R	*tha sin ^ceart gu \leòr*
		that's all right
16	Maggie	sixty one sixty two sixty three sixty four .hhh
17	Isabel	sixty *còig* sixty *sia* sixty *seachd* sixty seven
		five six seven
18	Maggie	I can ac- I can actually (.) eh count to one hundred in /Gaelic
19	Nana	^m
20	R	**HI**< ^hm
21	Isabel	*dè?*
		what?
22	Maggie	I can do more than a hundred in Gaelic

In this example, it appears that Maggie understands Isabel's question to be an implicit request to perform Gaelic rather than to use it in continuing to determine how many pupils are in her classes at the *Fèis* (as there certainly are not 60 pupils in each class). As discussed in Smith-Christmas (2016), this particular performance activity is well-ingrained within family practices, as from an early age, Maggie exhibited a propensity for counting in Gaelic. Within the 2009 corpus there are three documented instances where caregivers explicitly encourage Maggie to count in Gaelic and in these instances, counting is treated as a discrete activity tangential to the ongoing interaction. Now that she is older, Maggie still engages in this performance ritual and it is clear to see she perceives the expectation for her to perform this task correctly: after she admits that she can count no higher in Gaelic (Turn 14), she then counters this with claims in Turns 18 and 22 that she can indeed count to more than a 100 in Gaelic. The expectation to perform correctly may also stem from the fact that maths skills such as counting are normally associated with the school and the object of most school activities after all is to supply the correct answer. Thus, Isabel's

SUPPORT, TRANSMISSION, EDUCATION AND TARGET VARIETIES

request for Maggie to use Gaelic in counting not only frames the language as an activity separate from normative language use, but it also subtly links the language to the school; it is further argued that Isabel is very aware of this link with school, as in an interview in December 2014, Isabel contends that the only reason Maggie's younger brother Jacob will count in Gaelic is 'because they're doing it in school'. As well, the fact that Maggie was often asked to engage in this particular type of performance when she was younger may further invoke the authoritative dimension of Isabel's request: Maggie may feel this activity is somewhat childish, which is again supported by reference to Jacob, as in the 2014 recordings there are several instances where the caregivers ask Jacob (who was four at the time) to count in Gaelic (cf. also Dunmore's (2015, p. 185) example of a GME-educated adult ascribing her low Gaelic use in part to her association of Gaelic with childhood and therefore feeling as if she were going 'backwards' by speaking Gaelic).

Another example of framing Gaelic as a performance occurs later on in the interaction. This particular instance follows from Maggie's statement that she does not speak Gaelic at home because she is 'not in school', which, as seen below, leads to an argument between Isabel and Maggie about whether or not Maggie is 'good at speaking Gaelic'. This argument then finally culminates in Isabel directing Maggie to speak Gaelic, as is also seen below:

Excerpt 2

1	Maggie	a::n::::d (0.5) I don't need to speak Gaelic all the time=
2	Isabel	=but you won't (.) be so good at speaking Gaelic if you don't speak it all the time
3	Maggie	yeah but I <u>am</u> good at speaking Gaelic
4	Isabel	well I don't <u>think</u> you are (.) I <u>never</u> hear you speaking Gaelic
5	Isabel	tell me something in Gaelic then
6	Maggie	what- what- what like?
7	Isabel	what you were doing today
8	Maggie	HI< but that's ^hard
9	Isabel	HI< /hm (because) you've got no Gaelic
10	Maggie	yes I/do
11	Isabel	@
12	Maggie	I /do
13	R	*dè bha thu dèanamh an-diugh?*
		what were you doing today?
14	Isabel	*(5.6) 'g ithe? (4/6) 'g òl?*=
		eating? drinking?
15	Maggie	=/hm (.) *an \toiseach* (2.1) *bha mi tighinn a-steach agus* (0.8)
		at first I was coming inside and
		°an uair sin bha mi dèanamh tin whistle
		then I was doing

In Turn 5 of this excerpt, Maggie is commanded to 'tell something' to Isabel in Gaelic. Maggie is clearly somewhat blindsided by this abstract notion of 'telling something' in Gaelic and it is entirely possible that she finds this 'hard' not necessarily from a linguistic standpoint, but that she struggles with the abstraction of the command. Given the context of the earlier argument (Turns 2–4) about whether or not Maggie is 'good at Gaelic', Isabel's request could be construed as a challenge and in Turn 9, Isabel appears to think that she has proven her point by the fact that Maggie characterises this challenge as 'hard'. However, Maggie does not give up easily and she embarks on a narration in Gaelic. What emerges from this example is that again, there appears to be a performance aspect to using Gaelic; Isabel's request for Maggie to 'tell something' in Gaelic is similar to the way a caregiver might instruct a child to recite the alphabet or a poem (or count, as we saw earlier). Not only does this request contribute to framing Gaelic as a performance (as opposed to simply *using* the language), but the fact that this request is deployed as a means for Isabel to win the argument compounds its authoritative nature.

It should be noted that Maggie speaks Gaelic only *after* the adults have used Gaelic in their prior turns; it is probably ironic to anyone looking at this transcript excerpt that the interaction takes place through the medium of English. It is argued that the fact that the conversation is *about* Gaelic but takes place through English also helps to underscore the framing of Gaelic as a performance: the actual 'talking' (cf. Fishman, 1996, p. 79) is in English while the 'performance' is in Gaelic. Further, Isabel's framing of Gaelic as something which Maggie can be 'good at' is reminiscent of a school context and specifically the child's aptitude for a particular subject. After all, the phrase 'good at English' is not usually used in conjunction with assessing a pupil's spoken use of their (home) language, but rather, their ability in English as a school subject. Gaelic, however, is framed as something which Maggie can be 'good at' instead of simply a language which she speaks and which is used in her home. Furthermore, Isabel's assertion in Turn 4 invokes authority as it implies that Isabel is in a position to critique Maggie's use of Gaelic, the irony of which is that Isabel uses English in making this criticism.

The association of Gaelic and authority through the link between Gaelic and the school is heightened later on in the interaction. Maggie is continuing her narration about her day at the *Fèis* while Nana and Màiri, who were out of the room earlier, have just returned. Isabel then informs them that 'we're getting a Gaelic lesson here with wee Maggie'. There is nothing, however, about Maggie's narration that is in any way lesson-like. Anything that could be construed as didactic has been instigated by Isabel, for example, when Isabel quizzes Maggie on the Gaelic lexical item *talla* ('hall') after Maggie uses the English equivalent in her narration. This characterisation of Gaelic use as a 'lesson' not only overtly frames Gaelic in a school context, but it also works to mark Maggie's everyday narrative in Gaelic as deviating from normal language practices. The next section will look at the other ways which Isabel, now with the help of Màiri, further achieves this particular framing and will discuss how this framing works against the overall goal of language revitalisation in the family.

De-normatising Gaelic and imposing a double-standard

Besides treating the use of Gaelic as a type of performance as seen in the last two examples, another way in which Isabel and Màiri 'de-normatise' – that is, treat the use of Gaelic as deviating from the normal 'unmarked' code choice (cf. Myers-Scotton, 1988) – is by their incredulous reactions to Maggie's use of Gaelic. After Isabel imparts to Nana and Màiri that 'we're getting a Gaelic lesson here with wee Maggie', Maggie continues telling about her day at the *Fèis*. As seen

SUPPORT, TRANSMISSION, EDUCATION AND TARGET VARIETIES

below, Màiri then interjects, claiming that she cannot believe that Maggie is speaking Gaelic:

Excerpt 3

1	Màiri	ach I don't believe it
2	Maggie	\what?
3	Màiri	*thusa*
		you
4	Maggie	*thusa: dè?*
		you what?
5	Màiri	*bruidhinn Gàidhlig*
		speaking Gaelic
6	Nana	[[*tha Gàidhlig*]
7	Maggie	[[yes]
8	Nana	**HI**< *tha Gàidhlig aig Màiri* ^*cuideachd*
		Màiri speaks Gaelic too
9	Maggie	**HI**< *bha mi /dìreach bruidhinn* (([broi:jn])) *Gàidhlig*
		I was just speaking Gaelic
10	Màiri	**HI**< ^o: /*bruidhinn* (([broijn])) *Gàidhlig*
		speaking Gaelic
11	Nana	**HI**< *bha i bruidhinn Gàidhlig 's bruidhinnidh i* [[*Gàidhlig*]
		she was speaking Gaelic and she will speak Gaelic

Màiri's first turn in this excerpt situates Maggie's use of Gaelic in the realm of the incredible; it is *un*believable that Maggie would speak Gaelic. After Maggie counters this assertion with *bha mi dìreach bruidhinn Gàidhlig* ('I was just speaking speaking Gaelic'), Màiri then teases Maggie, imitating her dipthong in the word *bruidhinn* (typically, older speakers in the Campbell family would use an [i] as the first vowel in this lexical item). Although the conversation is very light-hearted, not only does Màiri's statement of disbelief mark Maggie's use of Gaelic as non-normative, but Màiri's imitation of Maggie's dipthong subtly marks the way that Maggie uses Gaelic as non-normative as well. This imitation also has the potential to act as a subtle critique of Maggie's linguistic capabilities in Gaelic, as Màiri appears to be implying that Maggie is not pronouncing the word *bruidhinn* correctly. Like Isabel's Turn 4 in Excerpt 2, Màiri's Turn 10 therefore also invokes some level of authority, as it implies that Màiri is in a position to critique Maggie's use of Gaelic. This in turn invokes a double-standard, as from eight years' of observing the Campbell family's linguistic practices, it is more 'unbelievable' to hear Màiri speaking Gaelic than it is to hear Maggie speaking Gaelic (see Smith-Christmas, 2012, 2014, 2016). This claim is further supported by the fact that in Turn 8 of Excerpt 3, Nana feels the need to point out that Màiri speaks Gaelic, which suggests that Nana thinks that Maggie does not even *know* that Màiri speaks Gaelic.

This concept of a double-standard is further emphasised later on in the interaction when Isabel congratulates Maggie on her use of Gaelic, remarking 'I didn't think you had any Gaelic actually until tonight at all – congratulations'. Not only does the congratulatory component of the utterance further frame Maggie's use of Gaelic as task-like in that it is something which appears can be *achieved*, but the preface to this congratulatory comment further marks Maggie's Gaelic use as non-normative. Like the previous example involving Màiri, the language choice used in making this implicit critique further implies a double standard, as Isabel is speaking English. Further, as previously mentioned, Isabel's daily use of Gaelic is also low overall and thus, by invoking a double-standard of Maggie, the caregivers in turn invoke some level of authority: the child must do what the adults wish her to do, even if it is not a practice in which they would habitually engage.

Isabel's requests for *monolingual* Gaelic further compound the double-standard nature of this interaction with Maggie. As discussed earlier, in Maggie's narration of her day at the *Fèis*, Isabel quizzed Maggie about the Gaelic equivalent of the word 'hall', thus implicitly requesting Maggie's use of monolingual Gaelic. Truly monolingual Gaelic, however, not only goes against the grain of Isabel's own language use, but that of her generation as well. When Isabel *does* speak Gaelic, she, like the other first generation members in this study, frequently insert English lexical items into otherwise-Gaelic speech. As I have argued elsewhere (see Smith-Christmas, 2012), the high degree of mixed language use is as much a facet of the older, traditional speakers in this study as is their fluency in Gaelic in comparison to younger speakers. This premise is even playfully illustrated in another part of this interaction: Maggie answers 'no, *cha robh*' (thus saying 'no' in both languages), and after much laughter and repetition of the phrase, Nana follows up Maggie's code-switched statement with '*sin mar a tha sinn* – code-switching, *nach e*, Cassie?' ('that's how we are – codewitching isn't it, Cassie?). Further, as evidenced by Isabel's use of mixed language use in the counting sequence in Excerpt 1 (Turns 6, 8 and 17), mixing is acceptable, even in a 'performance' such as counting. Thus, by requesting monolingual Gaelic use, in addition to framing Gaelic as non-normative practice in other parts of the interaction, here Isabel further de-normatises Maggie's Gaelic use by requesting a practice (monolingual Gaelic use) that in many ways goes against the grain of community and family usage norms.

In looking at the ways in which Maggie's use of Gaelic is framed as non-normative linguistic practice, it is argued that what Isabel and Màiri are actually doing is unwittingly *normalising* language shift and therefore contributing to its perpetuation. Although ostensibly Isabel and Màiri *think* their playful chidings, as well as subtle and not-so-subtle challenges to use the language, encourage Maggie to use more Gaelic, I contend that these actions in fact, on some level, further inhibit Maggie's use of her minority language. In exclaiming their surprise at Maggie's use of Gaelic, Isabel and Màiri orient to discourses that treat it as the standard that children, both within their own family and within Skye, do not speak Gaelic. Further, through their framings of Gaelic as a performance and a 'lesson', they also normalise another aspect of the language shift and revitalisation in Skye: that the one place the children *will* speak Gaelic is in the classroom context. The following section examines the implications of this reality in terms of language policy and planning, especially in terms of education as a language revitalisation strategy.

Discussion: implications for education in RLS

Earlier, I mentioned that this interaction was in part borne out of the Observer's Paradox; in knowing that they were under scrutiny, certain actors, namely Isabel and Màiri, behave differently than they normally would. Also, as previously mentioned, this interaction took place on the last night of several days and nights of recordings and up until now Maggie has spoken very little Gaelic. It would be easy, therefore, to see this interaction as the caregivers' attempts to prove to the researcher that Maggie can indeed speak Gaelic. However, although I think that this may influence the interaction on some level, I believe that the caregivers' stances are primarily ideologically driven and that my main role in the Observer's Paradox has been to bring latent pro-Gaelic ideologies to the forefront of family consciousness. Both Màiri and Isabel have made comments to me over the years which indicate that they desire to see Gaelic maintained, especially within their own family, and I believe the stances they take in this interaction are indicative of this pro-Gaelic ideology. However, when this ideology is juxtaposed with their habitual language practices, there appears to be a mismatch. As Dauenhauer and Dauenhauer (1998) and King (2000) demonstrate, this type of mismatch is not uncommon in minority language contexts, as pro-minority language ideologies are often pitted against mainstream-oriented ideologies which devalue the language. In the case of Isabel and Màiri, I contend that this accounts in part for both speakers' relatively low use of the language despite taking very pro-Gaelic stances in this particular interaction. The question remains, however: why do Isabel and Màiri's pro-Gaelic stances take such seemingly critical and didactic forms?

In attempting to answer this question, I will draw on the observation that certain Campbell family members take the ideological stance that GME should be doing more to reverse the language shift present in the third generation. Several times either Nana or Isabel have said to the children something to the effect of 'You go to a Gaelic school, therefore you should speak Gaelic' (Smith-Christmas, 2016), a decree clearly reminiscent of John MacNamara's story mentioned in the introduction. This also surfaces in an interview with Nana, Isabel and Seumas (Nana's son) in December 2014, in which Seumas postulates that he might have become a more frequent user of Gaelic if GME had been available when he had gone to school. In Nana and Isabel's view, one of the reasons for the language's decline within their own generation, as well as Nana's children's generation, is the lack of education available in Gaelic when they were school-aged. This is one of the reasons that Nana ascribes to Isabel's relatively low use of Gaelic in comparison to Nana's: Isabel never attained literacy in the language and at some level, this disenfranchisement has impacted her language use. Nana also attributes her own children's habitual use of English to its status as the language of instruction in school: Nana's first child was a Gaelic monoglot in his early years and in Nana's words, 'brought home the English' from school. In Nana, Isabel's and perhaps even Màiri's view, therefore, it seems logical that once this educational lacuna was filled, the language decline would be stemmed. These particular speakers are not alone in their logic; as Dunmore (in press) points out, there is a clear assumed link between GME and RLS, encapsulated recently, for example, by a Consultation Paper on the GME Bill, which reads (2014, p. 3):

> The Scottish Government's aim is to create a secure future for Gaelic in Scotland. This will only be achieved by an increase in the numbers of those learning, speaking and using the language. Gaelic medium education can make an important contribution to this, both in terms of young people's language learning but also in terms of the effects this can have on language use in home, community and workplace.

However, not even taking other studies and families into account, it is clear to see from the Campbell family that a disconnect exists between education in the minority language and use of the minority language outside the confines of the school. Returning to the question of why Isabel and Màiri's chidings take such seemingly critical and didactic stances, it appears that part of what they may actually be doing, especially in the case of Isabel, is implicitly critiquing this disconnect between minority language use in the school and its (lack of) use in other domains such as the home. Coincidentally, the form this critique takes is very didactic in its delivery and is reminiscent of the place in which, because of revitalisation efforts, Maggie uses the most Gaelic: the school. These negative framings therefore may be in part an exercise in blame-shifting; here, the blame is either placed on the child or on the school instead on the caregivers' own language practices (cf. Kroskrity's, 2009, p. 50 analysis of a similar stance in the Tewa community: 'the in-progress language shift is misrecognized not as a failure of parents and community but rather as a failure of the children'). However, although blame-shifting may play some role in what is going on in this particular interaction, I contend that these framings are also suggestive of what Costa (2013) characterises as the abstraction of 'language' in RLS efforts, where language is often treated as an object, separate from the *people* speaking the language. We see this in Isabel and Màiri's attempt at language revitalisation at the microlevel: their didactic framings reify Gaelic as an object, not something that is a part of normal, everyday communication. Further, what happens is that 'speaking' a language permutates into *performing* a language and the fact that this permutation occurs reflects the advanced state of shift in the Campbell family: although many of the Campbell family members such as Isabel and Màiri *can* (and sometimes *do*) speak Gaelic, the language exists mostly in abstraction. Gaelic is *something* Isabel and Màiri wish to *save* (i.e. to pass on to the third generation), the irony of which of course is that the caregivers' own language practices are part of the reason why the language needs 'saving' in the family in the first place (see Smith-Christmas, 2014, 2016). Similarly, the fact that Gaelic is largely absent from normative language use in the community but exists in the school compounds this abstraction: Gaelic is parcelled up according to domain instead of existing as an integrated part of community life. This of course is simply a reality of language shift and pointing out these realities is not intended to denigrate RLS efforts, either in the Campbell family or in the wider community, but rather, to highlight that while children like Maggie may be given the linguistic tools and opportunity to use their minority language, what seems to be absent is the *desire* to use the language outside the confines of the educational context (cf. Strubell's, 2001 Catherine Wheel model; also Harris, 2005, p. 974 as mentioned in the introduction). The desire, or rather lack of it, therefore, is one of the missing links in language planning and one of the reasons why the domains may not necessarily work in tandem as those involved in RLS intend. Again drawing on Costa (2013), what is needed, therefore, is a deeper understanding of speakers' sociohistorical trajectories; their own roles in language shift and maintenance; and, in this particular case, how the association of the language with a particular authoritative domain can potentially inhibit the use of the minority language.

This is not to say however that GME has not had a positive effect on Maggie; for example, the fact that Maggie's experience with literacy has primarily been through the medium of Gaelic means that she will happily read and write in Gaelic. One day, Maggie may choose to change her linguistic practices and GME will have contributed to her linguistic ability to enact this change (cf. Pujolar & Puigdevall's, 2015 concept of linguistic *mudes*). The point to be made here is that although immersion language education can be a valuable tool in RLS, there is not necessarily a correspondence between the pupils' *learning* of the language and *using* the language, and that other factors, such as the affective associations (e.g. authority) that this language-domain relationship may take on, need to be brought into scope. This point is certainly not a new one within

SUPPORT, TRANSMISSION, EDUCATION AND TARGET VARIETIES

RLS research, but it is nonethless important to see how this reality unfolds at the microlevel and how it relates to the reflexive nature of language shift in the home and the community. It is hoped that a deeper understanding of this reality may contribute to effective language planning, especially in terms of the role of education in RLS.

Notes

1. This quote is from Fishman (1996, p. 79). Full reference given in References section.
2. This is a pseudonym, as are all names used in this study.
3. For both corpora, each speakers' turns in the conversation were coded for language: monolingual Gaelic, monolingual English, mixed (i.e. code-switching) and undecided. For the first generation speakers, in many cases the insertion of single lexical items into otherwise Gaelic utterances were coded as 'Mononlingual Gaelic'. due to the proliferation of English lexical items into everyday Gaelic discourse (see Smith-Christmas, 2012).
4. A further 5% were coded as 'Mixed'. No turns were coded as 'Undecided'.

Acknowledgements

The author thanks the organisers of the Celtic Sociolinguistics Symposium for the invitation to speak at such a stimulating conference and to the audience for their insightful comments. The author would also thank the two anonymous reviewers for their helpful comments and also to Dr Stuart Dunmore for transcribing this interaction and for his many helpful insights on GME and RLS. The writing of this article has benefitted from ongoing discussions on the themes of 'new speakers' as part of the COST EU Action IS1306 entitled, 'New Speakers in a Multilingual Europe: Opportunities and Challenges'. All mistakes are of course my own.

Disclosure statement

No potential conflict of interest was reported by the authors.

Funding

Thanks to Soillse for funding this research.

Transcription conventions used

:	Elongated sound
-	Cut-off
<u>word</u>	Emphasis
WORD	Increased amplitude
°	Decreased amplitude
HI<	Higher pitch
WH<	Whispered
CR<	Creaky voice
BR<	Breathy voice
> <	Accelerated speech
=	Latching speech
[[ ]	Overlapping speech
(.5)	Pause (seconds)
(.)	Micropause (less than two-tenths of a second)
@	Laughter (pulse)
(( ))	Non-verbal action

SUPPORT, TRANSMISSION, EDUCATION AND TARGET VARIETIES

{ }   Word/sound said ingressively
/   Rising pitch
\   Falling pitch
∧   Rise/fall pitch
.hh   Egressive sound
(?)   Uncertainty in transcript
•   Turns omitted

References

Armstrong, T. (2013). *Negotiating interactional spaces: The playground as a bridge between language in the school and in the home.* Paper presented at the BAAL/Cambridge University Press Seminar, Lews Castle College UHI.

Armstrong, T. C. (2014). Naturalism and ideological work: How is family language policy renegotiated as both parents and children learn a threatened minority language? *International Journal of Bilingual Education and Bilingualism, 17*(5), 570–585.

Auer, P. (1984). *Bilingual conversation.* Amsterdam: Johns Benjamins.

Baker, C. (2007). Becoming bilingual through bilingual education. In P. Auer & L. Wei (Eds.), *Handbook of multilingualism and multilingual communication* (pp. 131–154). Berlin: Mouton de Gruyter.

Clague, M. (2009). Cross-linguistic discourse markers in Manx Gaelic and English. In *Proceedings of the Harvard Celtic Colloquium Vol. 24/25 (2004/2005)* (pp. 195–205). Cambridge, MA: Department of Celtic Languages and Literatures, Harvard University.

Costa, J. (2013). Language endangerment and revitalisation as elements of regimes of truth: Shifting terminology to shift perspective. *Journal of Multilingual and Multicultural Development, 34*(4), 317–331.

Dauenhauer, N. M., & Dauenhauer, R. (1998). Technical, emotional, and ideological issues in reversing language shift: Examples from Southeast Alaska. In L. A. Grenoble & L. J. Whaley (Eds.), *Endangered languages: Language loss and community response* (pp. 57–98). Cambridge: Cambridge University Press.

Dunmore, S. (2015). *Bilingual life after school? Language use, ideologies, and attitudes among gaelic-medium educated adults* (Unpublished Ph.D. thesis). University of Edinburgh.

Dunmore, S. (in press). New Gaelic speakers, New Gaels? Language ideologies and ethnolinguistic continuity among Gaelic-medium educated adults. In C. Smith-Christmas, Ó. Murchadha, N. Hornsby, & M. Moriarty (Eds.), *New speakers of minority languages: Linguistic ideologies and practices.* Basingstoke: Palgrave MacMillan.

Edwards, V., & Newcombe, L. P. (2005). When school is not enough: New initiatives in intergenerational language transmission in Wales. *International Journal of Bilingual Education and Bilingualism, 8*(4), 298–312.

Fishman, J. A. (1991). *Reversing language shift.* Clevedon: Multilingual Matters.

Fishman, J. A. (1996). What do you lose when you lose your language. In G. Cantoni (Ed.), *Stabilizing indigenous languages* (pp. 71–81). Flagstaff: University of Northern Arizona.

Fishman, J. A. (2001). *Can threatened languages be saved? Reversing language shift revisited: A twenty-first century perspective.* Clevedon: Multilingual Matters.

Galloway, J. M. K. (2012). *Gaelic education data 2011–12.* Inverness: Bòrd na Gàidhlig.

Harris, J. (2005). The role of ordinary primary schools in the maintenance and revival of Irish. In J. Cohen, K. McAlister, K. Rolstad, & J. MacSwan (Eds.), *ISB4: Proceedings of the 4th international symposium on bilingualism* (pp. 977–964). Somerville, MA: Cascadilla Press.

Highland Council/Comhairle na Gàidhealtachd Website. (2015). *Gaelic in schools.* Retrieved from: http://www.highland.gov.uk/info/878/schools/18/gaelic_medium_education

Hodges, R. (2009). Welsh language use among young people in the Rhymney Valley. *Contemporary Wales, 22*, 16–35.

Hornberger, N. (Ed.). (2008). *Can schools save indigenous languages? Policy and Practice on four continents.* Basingstoke: Palgrave Macmillan.

King, K. A. (2000). Language ideologies and heritage language education. *International Journal of Bilingual Education and Bilingualism, 3*(3), 167–184.

Kroskrity, P. (2009). Narrative reproductions: Ideologies of storytelling, authoritative words, and generic regimentation in the village of Tewa. *Journal of Linguistic Anthropology, 19*(1), 40–56.

MacKinnon, K. (1974). *The lion's tongue: The original and continuing language of the Scottish people.* Inverness: Club Leabhar.

MacLeod, D. J. (2003). An historical overview. In M. Nicolson & M. MacIver (Eds.), *Gaelic medium education* (pp. 1–14). Edinburgh: Dunedin Academic Press.

McLeod, W. (2003). Gaelic medium education in Scotland. In M. Scott & N. B. Roise (Eds.), *Gaelic-medium education provision: Northern Ireland, the Republic of Ireland, Scotland and Isle of man* (pp. 104–132). Belfast: Clo Ollscoil na Banriona.

Meek, B. A. (2007). Respecting the language of elders: Ideological shift and linguistic discontinuity in a Northern Athapascan community. *Journal of Linguistic Anthropology, 17*(1), 23–43.

Morrison, M. F. (2006). A' Chiad Ghinealach- The first generation: A survey of Gaelic- medium education in the Western Isles. In W. McLeod (Ed.), *Revitalising Gaelic in Scotland* (pp. 139–154). Edinburgh: Dunedin Academic Press.

Müller, M. (2006). Language use, language attitudes, and Gaelic writing ability among secondary pupils in the Isle of Skye. In W. McLeod (Ed.), *Revitalising Gaelic in Scotland* (pp. 119–138). Edinburgh: Dunedin Academic Press.

Myers-Scotton, C. (1988). Code-switching as indexical of social negotiations. In L. Wei (Ed.), *The bilingualism reader* (2000th ed., pp. 151–186). London: Routledge.

Nance, C. (2013). *Phonetic variation, sound change, and identity in Scottish Gaelic* (Unpublished Ph.D. thesis). University of Glasgow.

National Records of Scotland (NROS). (2013). *Statistical bulletin- release 2A.* Retrieved from http://www.scotlandscensus.gov.uk/documents/censusresults/release2a/Stats

Ó Baoill, D. (2007). Origins of Irish-medium education: The dynamic core of language revitalisation in Northern Ireland. *International Journal of Bilingual Education and Bilingualism, 10*, 410–427.

O'Hanlon, F. (2010). Gaelic-medium primary education in Scotland: Toward a new taxonomy? In G. Munro & I. Mac an Tàilleir (Eds.), *Coimhearsnachd na Gàidhlig an-Diugh/Gaelic Communities today* (pp. 99–116). Edinburgh: Dunedin.

O'Hanlon, F., McLeod, W., & Paterson, L. (2010). *Gaelic-medium education in Scotland: Choice and attainment at the primary and early secondary school stages.* Inverness: Bòrd na Gàidhlig.

Ó hIfearnáin, T. (2011). Breton language maintenance and regeneration in regional education policy. In C. Norrby & J. Hajek (Eds.), *Uniformity and diversity in language policy* (pp. 93–106). Bristol: Multilingual Matters.

Pujolar, J., & Puigdevall, M. (2015). Linguistic mudes: How to become a new speaker in Catalonia. *International Journal of the Sociology of Language, 2015*(231), 167–187.

Robertson, B. (2003). Gaelic education. In T. Bryce, W. Humes, D. Gillies, & A. Kennedy (Eds.), *Scottish Education* (pp. 250–261). Edinburgh: Edinburgh University Press.

Scottish Government. (2014). *Consultation paper on a gaelic medium education bill.* Retrieved from: http://www.gov.scot/Resource/0045/00454897.pdf

Smith-Christmas, C. (2012). *I've lost it here de a bh' agam: Language shift, maintenance, and code-switching in a bilingual family* (Unpublished PhD thesis). University of Glasgow.

Smith-Christmas, C. (2014). Being socialised in language shift: The impact of extended family members on family language policy. *Journal of Multilingual and Multicultural Development, 35*(5), 511–526. doi:10.1080/01434632.2014.882930

Smith-Christmas, C. (2016). *Family language policy: Maintaining an endangered language in the home.* Basingstoke: Palgrave Macmillan.

Smith-Christmas, C., & Armstrong, T. C. (2014). Complementary reversing language shift strategies in education: The importance of adult heritage learners of threatened minority languages. *Current Issues in Language Planning, 15*(3), 312–326.

Spolsky, B. (1991). Hebrew language revitalization within a general theory of second language learning. In *Influence of language on culture and thought: Essays in honor of Joshua A. fishman's sixty-fifth birthday* (pp. 136–156). Berlin: Walter de Gruyter.

SUPPORT, TRANSMISSION, EDUCATION AND TARGET VARIETIES

Strubell, M. (2001). Catalan a Decade Later. In J. A. Fishman (Ed.), *Can threatened languages be saved? Reversing language shift, revisited: A twenty-first century perspective* (pp. 260–283). Clevedon: Multilingual Matters.

Will, V. K. A. (2012). *Why Kenny can't can: The language socialization experiences of gaelic-medium educated children in Scotland* (Unpublished Ph.D. thesis). University of Michigan.

Woolard, K. (2011). Is there linguistic life after high school? Longitudinal changes in the bilingual repertoire in metropolitan Barcelona. *Language in Society, 40*, 617–648.

Factors influencing the likelihood of choice of Gaelic-medium primary education in Scotland: results from a national public survey

Fiona O'Hanlon ⑩ and Lindsay Paterson

ABSTRACT

This paper investigates the factors influencing the likelihood of choice of Gaelic-medium primary education in Scotland by means of the analysis of a national survey of public attitudes conducted in 2012. Binary logistic regression is used to investigate the association of five dimensions found in previous literature to be associated with the choice of Scottish Gaelic-medium education: (i) demographic characteristics, (ii) exposure to Gaelic, (iii) cultural and national identities, (iv) views on the future of Gaelic and (v) views on Gaelic in education. The present research found views about Gaelic in education and views on the future of Gaelic to have the greatest explanatory power in predicting likelihood of choice of Gaelic-medium education, for demographic characteristics and 'cultural and national identities' to have substantial explanatory power, and for exposure to Gaelic to have low explanatory power. The paper uses Baker's three contexts for the growth of bilingual education in Wales – bilingual education as language planning, as pedagogy and as politics – as its explanatory framework, and shows that these three contexts also underpin the potential growth of Gaelic-medium education in Scotland. Potential implications for policy and for methodological approaches to studying choice of bilingual education are presented.

1. Introduction

Baker (2000) argues three contexts to have underpinned the rapid expansion of Welsh-medium primary schooling between the mid- and late twentieth century: bilingual education as Language Planning, as Pedagogy and as Politics. The first considers the incorporation of Welsh within the education system from the perspective of the vitality of the language itself – in particular, the contribution that Welsh-medium education can make to acquisition, usage, status and corpus planning for Welsh (Welsh Language Board, 1999; Cooper, 1989). The second views bilingual education as effective pedagogy – as both a culturally appropriate form of child-centred education for first-language Welsh pupils, and as an effective means of developing bilingualism, bi-literacy and an appreciation of more than one culture for all pupils. International evidence on attainment benefits of early immersion bilingual education and of the cognitive benefits of well-developed bilingualism are also cited in this regard (Bamford & Mizokawa, 1991; Genesee, 1983; Ricciardelli, 1992). The third context – bilingual education as politics – takes a broader societal view relating to public perceptions of the place of Welsh in the cultural heritage of Wales and in national identity, and to a public willingness to accept bilingual education in Welsh and English as an option in educational policy in Wales. Such contexts for growth have been reflected in research on parental rationales for the choice of Welsh-medium education (Bellin, Farrell, Higgs, & White, 1999; Bush, Atkinson, & Read, 1981; Hodges, 2012; Packer & Campbell, 1997; Thomas, 2013; Williams, Roberts, & Isaac, 1978), and also in research on parental rationales for the choice of Irish-medium education (Kavanagh, 2013; Maguire, 1991; Mas-Moury Mack, 2013; Ó Riagáin & Ó Glasáin, 1979; Ó Donnagáin, 1995).

The present paper investigates the extent to which Baker's three contexts also serve as contexts for the growth of Gaelic-medium education in Scotland, where the provision of early total immersion education has grown from two primary schools teaching 24 pupils in 1985 to 59 primary schools teaching 2818 pupils in 2014 (Baker, 2011; Galloway, 2015; MacLeod, 2003). This question is investigated by means of a national survey in Scotland in 2012 (ScotCen Social Research 2013a): specifically, we investigate what characteristics and views are associated with the respondent's saying that they would be likely to choose Gaelic-medium primary education for a child of their own. The aim of the paper is threefold: (i) to better understand the factors associated with the likelihood of choice of Gaelic-medium primary education in Scotland, as compared with factors reported in previous research on enacted choice of Gaelic-medium education, (ii) to explore the extent to which Baker's (2000) three contexts for the growth of Welsh-medium education also underpin potential growth of Gaelic-medium education in Scotland and (iii) to encourage the collection of key demographic information about respondents in future research on parental choice of early immersion bilingual education in order to better facilitate cross-national comparisons.

2. Contextual background

2.1. Policy for parental choice of Gaelic-medium education

Parental choice of Gaelic-medium primary education is facilitated by means of provisions made in the 1980 and 1981 *Education (Scotland) Acts*. The 1980 Act states that 'pupils are to be educated in accordance with the wishes of their parents', whilst the 1981 Act enables parents to request that their child attend a particular school within a local authority area. Such provisions have underpinned the growth of Gaelic-medium primary education over the last 35 years, with parental requests for new Gaelic-medium primary provision being negotiated between parents and individual local authorities according to individual local authority processes and criteria. In the 2014–2015 school year, Gaelic-medium primary education was provided in 14 of the 32 Local Authority areas in Scotland, with 13 further local authorities having established cross-boundary agreements with neighbouring local authorities to facilitate parental choice of Gaelic-medium primary education, rather than establishing such provision in their area. Nationally, in the 2014–2015 academic year, Gaelic-medium education was available in 59 of Scotland's primary schools (2.9% of the total), and 2818 primary pupils attend Gaelic-medium provision (0.7% of the total) (Galloway, 2015).

However, the *Education (Scotland) Act*, passed by the Scottish Parliament in February 2016, marks a change in the policy context, as it establishes a *national* statutory process by which parents can request the establishing of new Gaelic-medium primary provision in their local area. Provided that there are at least five pupils in the same pre-school year group within an area whose parents wish them to be educated in Gaelic-medium education, the local authority must investigate the feasibility of providing such an education, and must provide it unless it is 'unreasonable' to do so in relation to considerations specified in the Bill (for details, see Section 10(6), *Education (Scotland) Bill 2016*). In addition, the Act requires each of the 32 Scottish education authorities to 'promote' the provision, or the potential for the provision, of Gaelic-medium primary education within their area. These measures – which command cross-party-political support – are framed as 'recognising, respecting and promoting children's and parents' rights' in relation to accessing Gaelic-medium education (Scottish Government, 2015a, p. 1), and are noted to reflect Scottish Government support for Gaelic-medium education as a means of promoting and maintaining the Gaelic language in Scotland (Scottish Government, 2015b).[1] Such a policy context encourages the establishment of new Gaelic-medium primary provision where parental demand exists. The present paper investigates the characteristics and views that may underpin such demand, by means of an investigation of the factors associated with the likelihood of choice of Gaelic-medium education.

2.2. Research on parental choice of Gaelic-medium education

Six studies have been published of the reasons for choice of Gaelic-medium education in Scotland (Johnstone, Harlen, MacNeil, Stradling, & Thorpe, 1999; MacNeil, 1993; O'Hanlon, 2015; O'Hanlon, McLeod, & Paterson, 2010; Stephen, McPake, McLeod, Pollock, & Carroll, 2010; Stockdale, MacGregor, & Munro, 2003). These studies, which have included 500 parents over a 25-year period, have identified two main rationales for choice – the first relating to linguistic and cultural heritage, and the second to education. The linguistic and cultural heritage rationale typically related to a desire that Gaelic-medium education continue a tradition of Gaelic-speaking, at the family, community, regional or national level. The education-based rationales typically related to the linguistic and cognitive outcomes associated with bilingual education, and to a perception that Gaelic-medium education is of good quality in terms of its pedagogical processes and context. Such rationales were present in all six studies. In addition, three studies identified demographic factors associated with Gaelic-medium parents. Johnstone et al. (1999, p. 2), using data from 1996–1998, noted the Gaelic-medium pupils in their survey to have lower levels of free-school meal entitlement than English-medium pupils, a socio-economic finding replicated in a study by O'Hanlon et al. (2010, p. 27) using data from 2006–2007, which found Gaelic-medium to have a lower proportion of pupils living in the 20% most deprived areas (as classified by the Scottish Index of Multiple Deprivation (SIMD)). The study by Stockdale et al. (2003, p. 39) also found a relationship between parental education level and choice of Gaelic-medium education, noting

SUPPORT, TRANSMISSION, EDUCATION AND TARGET VARIETIES

that parents educated to degree level or to upper secondary school were more likely to choose Gaelic-medium education for their child. Of the previous research, the Stockdale et al. (2003) survey was the most methodologically similar to the present one, being based on a questionnaire survey and statistical modelling of the factors associated with the choice of Gaelic-medium education. In addition to parental education level, the research found four further factors to be associated with the choice of Gaelic-medium education: parental competence in Gaelic, positive parental opinion of Gaelic and of Gaelic-medium education, migration to a Gaelic-speaking area, and a child's maternal grandmother being a Gaelic-speaker.

The present research aimed to incorporate the contexts identified by Baker (2000) and the factors identified by the previous literature in the Scottish context into a module of questions designed for inclusion in the *2012 Scottish Social Attitudes Survey*. Five 'dimensions' of interest were identified based on previous research, relating to (i) demographic characteristics, (ii) exposure to Gaelic, (iii) perceptions of the place of Gaelic in cultural and national identity, (iv) views of Gaelic in education and (v) views about the future of Gaelic. The questions included within each dimension are outlined in Section 3.1. Where possible, survey questions drew on previous attitudinal research regarding lesser-used Celtic languages (Scotland: Bird, 1993; MacKinnon, 1981, 1995; Market Research UK, 2003; Scottish Government, 2011; Stockdale et al., 2003; Ireland: Ó Riagáin, 1997, 2007; Wales: Cole & Williams, 2004; Welsh Language Board, 1995). The survey questions were additionally shaped by the comments of an expert advisory panel of academics and policy-makers from Scotland, Wales and Ireland, and by the feedback of 51 adults involved in a pilot study.

This paper investigates the effects of these five dimensions and their associated variables on the likelihood of choice of Gaelic-medium education. The 'likelihood of choice' was investigated by means of a survey question (detailed in Table 1) that asked respondents how likely they would be to send a child of their own to Gaelic-medium education,

Table 1. Likelihood of choice of Gaelic-medium primary education for own child.

	Percentage
Very likely	11
Fairly likely	17
Not very likely	28
Not at all likely	44
Sample size	963

Notes: Percentages are weighted; sample size is unweighted.
The question asked was: 'In some parts of Scotland, parents can choose to send their child to a primary school where most of the lessons are in Gaelic. For example, children would be taught maths or history in Gaelic rather than in English. If there was a primary school in **this** area where most of the lessons were in Gaelic, how likely would you be to send a child of your own to this school instead of a school where all the lessons are in English?'. The response options are those shown above. Respondents were encouraged by interviewers to provide an answer to this question even if they were not parents, or if their own children were grown up. In such cases, they were asked to think about how they would feel about this educational option if they did have primary-school-aged children.

if Gaelic-medium education was available in their area. The question aimed to index 'behavioural intentions' (Ajzen, 1991, p. 181), which, within the theory of planned behaviour, is the respondent's intention in relation to a certain behaviour, taking into consideration their attitudes towards it, social norms, and the extent to which the respondent feels that they might be able to enact such a behaviour (Ajzen, 1991). The paper investigates two key research questions:

(i) Within each of the dimensions identified in previous research as being important to the choice of Gaelic-medium education, which variables are statistically significantly associated with likelihood of choice of Gaelic-medium education?

(ii) When the impact of all five dimensions is considered together, which dimensions have the largest influence on the choice of Gaelic-medium education, and, within this, which individual variables retain statistical significance?

The discussion will consider the findings in relation to previous literature, and in relation to Baker's (2000) framework of bilingual education as language planning, as pedagogy and as politics, in order to explore the extent to which these three contexts can also be seen to underpin potential growth of Gaelic-medium education in Scotland.

3. Data and methods

3.1. Data

The data were collected as part of the Scottish Social Attitudes Survey of 2012 (ScotCen Social Research, 2013a). The survey aimed to obtain a representative sample of adults aged 18 or over who were living in Scotland in the summer of 2012. It used a multi-stage clustered probability design. The first stage involved selecting 87 postcode sectors. In urban areas, these were selected with probability proportional to the number of addresses, and in rural areas they were selected with probability proportional to twice the number of addresses. The postcode sectors were stratified according to the Scottish Government urban–rural classification, by region and by percentage of household heads in non-manual occupations (Socio-Economic Groups 1–6 and 13, taken from the 2001 Census). The second stage of sampling involved the random selection of 28 addresses from each postcode sector. The third stage involved interviewers randomly selecting one adult to interview at each address. In total, 1229 interviews were conducted, a response rate of 54%. The achieved sample was weighted to match the age-and-sex structure of the population, and also to correct for over-sampling of rural areas, differential selection probabilities of respondents by household-size, and patterns of non-response (for more details, see ScotCen Social Research, 2013b). The representativeness of the sample can be assessed in relation to other, larger, surveys. For example, the weighted sample had a distribution of highest educational attainment that was close to that found by the much larger Scottish Household Survey of 2011, had levels of party-political support representative of that in the May 2012 elections to Scottish local councils, and had a proportion of Gaelic speakers of 1.1%, the same as the 1.1% reported in the 2011 Census.

The questionnaire in the survey contained 40 questions relating to Gaelic, in addition to questions on many other topics (for details see ScotCen Social Research, 2013b). It also contained questions on general demographic information, such as age, sex and occupation, and on personal national identity. The questionnaire was administered by face-to-face interviewing within the respondent's home, along with a laptop-based self-completion section for questions that were particularly sensitive. Respondents were offered the option of completing the module of questions on Gaelic in Gaelic (by means of a pre-recorded version of the questions on a laptop): none chose to do so.

The present paper uses the information in the survey to explore the factors associated with the likelihood of sending a child to Gaelic-medium primary education. The explanatory variables included in the analysis (detailed below) represent the five dimensions which are known from previous research to be associated with the choice of Gaelic-medium education. Respondents with missing data on any of the explanatory variables or on the dependent variable were omitted, leaving data from 963 respondents (78% of the full sample). Descriptive statistics presented in this section are weighted percentage distributions based on this usable sample.

3.1.1. Dependent variable

Table 1 shows the question asked of respondents on the likelihood of choice of Gaelic-medium primary education, and the pattern of response across the 963 respondents.

This variable constitutes the dependent variable in the logistic regression analysis described in Section 3.2. For the analysis, the variable was made dichotomous – with one category consisting of the 28% of respondents who were 'very' or 'fairly' likely to choose Gaelic-medium education), and the other consisting of the 72% of respondents who were 'not very' or 'not at all' likely to do so.[2]

3.1.2. Explanatory variables

The explanatory variables included in the analysis related to respondents' (i) demographic characteristics, (ii) exposure to Gaelic, (iii) cultural and national identities, (iv) views on the future of Gaelic and (v) views on Gaelic in education. Variables relating to each of these five dimensions were selected for inclusion in the statistical models by means of a two-stage process. Firstly, all variables relating to the dimensions of interest available within the Scottish Social Attitudes Survey were listed and the relationship between the potential explanatory variables and the dependent variable was individually tested using chi-squared tests for categorical variables, and t-tests for continuous variables. Only variables which had a statistically significant relationship with the dependent variable at the 10% significance level were considered for entry into the models. The potential explanatory variables within each dimension were then explored (using correlation and logistic regression) to ensure that they were measuring different phenomena. In cases in which two or more variables were shown to be measuring similar phenomena, an indicator variable was chosen for the modelling, or a scale conducted from several variables. The variables selected for inclusion in the analysis are described below. The appendix[3] contains a summary of the additional variables that were considered for inclusion.

SUPPORT, TRANSMISSION, EDUCATION AND TARGET VARIETIES

(i) *Demographic factors*

Three variables were included in the modelling:

- Age – with categories: 18–24 (12%), 25–34 (18%), 35–44 (17%), 45–54 (18%), 55–64 (16%), 65+ (19%).
- Highest educational qualification – with categories: tertiary (38%), upper secondary (22%), middle secondary (24%), none (16%).
- Level of social and economic deprivation of local area (with five equal-sized parts: from the 20% least deprived areas in Scotland to the 20% most deprived areas in Scotland), based on the Scottish Index of Multiple Deprivation (Scottish Government, 2009). (1 = most deprived (20%), 2 (21%), 3 (19%), 4 (18%), 5 = least deprived (22%).[4]

Neither sex nor whether the respondent had children of school age were found to be associated with likelihood of choice of Gaelic-medium education.

(ii) *Exposure to Gaelic*

Three variables were included in the modelling:

- Competence in understanding Gaelic – with response categories: none (72.7%), the odd word (24.1%), a few simple sentences (2.0%), parts of conversations (0.3%), most conversations (0.5%) and all conversations (0.4%). The latter four categories were grouped into a single category 'more than the odd word'.
- Exposure to Gaelic in the last 12 months – a derived variable which represents an average of a respondent's exposure to Gaelic in five contexts – (i) on TV/Radio, (ii) in the street/public place, (iii) in the home, (iv) on road or public signs and (v) through singing – over the last 12 months. Respondents were asked to report their exposure to Gaelic in each context on a 5-point scale, from 1 = never, to 5 = more than once a week. The mean of the five items was taken to form a scale of exposure to Gaelic in the last 12 months, with high values indicating frequent exposure. Distribution: 1–1.99 (66%), 2–2.99 (29%), 3–3.99 (4%), 4–4.99 (1%).
- Exposure to Gaelic in childhood (scale recording respondents' reported exposure to Gaelic in childhood where 1 = no exposure and 6 = daily exposure). Distribution: 1 = no exposure (83%), 2 = less than once a month (6%), 3 = more than once a month (3%), 4 = about once per week (3%), 5 = more than once per week (2%), 1 = every day (3%).

(iii) *National and cultural identity*

Four variables were included in the modelling:

- National identity – with response categories: Scottish not British (23%), more Scottish than British (33%), equally Scottish and British (29%), more British than Scottish (6%), British not Scottish (4%), Other (5%).

54

SUPPORT, TRANSMISSION, EDUCATION AND TARGET VARIETIES

- Perceived importance of Gaelic to respondent's own cultural heritage – scale with 1 = not at all important (35%), 2 = not very important (34%), 3 = can't choose (5%), 4 = fairly important (18%) and 5 = very important (8%).
- Perceived importance of Gaelic to the cultural heritage of the Highlands and Islands.[5] Scale as above, 1 = not at all important (2%), 2 (7%), 3 (3%), 4 (37%), 5 = very important (51%).
- Perceived importance of Gaelic to the cultural heritage of Scotland. Scale as above, 1 = not at all important (4%), 2 (16%), 3 (3%), 4 (45%), 5 = very important (32%).

(iv) *Views about the future of Gaelic*

Four variables were included in the modelling:

- Respondents' views on encouraging the use of Gaelic in Scotland – with categories: should not be encouraged at all (11%), should be encouraged in areas where it is already spoken (55%), should be encouraged everywhere in Scotland (34%).
- Respondents' expectations regarding the number of Gaelic speakers in Scotland in 50 years' time – with categories: fewer people than now (55%), about the same number of people as now (31%), more people than now (14%).
- Respondents' preferences regarding how many Gaelic speakers there will be in Scotland in 50 years' time – with categories: fewer people than now (12%), about the same number as now (41%), more people than now (47%).
- Respondents' views on the level of public spending on Gaelic, with respondents being told that current annual expenditure was about £24 million, or £4.80 for each person in Scotland. Categories: too much money (33%), about the right amount of money (47%), too little money (20%).

(v) *Gaelic in education*

Six variables were included in the modelling, with two variables indexing each of the three contexts within Baker's (2000) framework.[6]

(i) Gaelic-medium education as pedagogy:
- *whether Gaelic-medium educated pupils 'do better at school' than English-medium educated pupils*; scale with 1 = strongly disagree and 5 = strongly agree). Response categories: 1 = strongly disagree (7%), 2 = disagree (27%), 3 = neither agree nor disagree/can't choose (57%), 4 = agree (8%), 5 = strongly agree (1%).
- *whether Gaelic-medium education is 'a bad thing because it separates children taught in Gaelic from children taught in English'*. Same response categories as above, 1 = strongly disagree (8%), 2 (47%), 3 (23%), 4 (19%), 5 = strongly agree (3%).

(ii) the value of learning Gaelic (which may be seen as relating to the public political debate about the importance of Gaelic in Scotland):
- *whether learning 'languages such as French is more useful than learning Gaelic'*. Same response categories as above, 1 = strongly disagree (4%), 2 (11%), 3 (28%), 4 (36%), 5 = strongly agree (21%).

- *whether 'learning the Gaelic language is pointless in the twenty-first century'.* Same response categories, 1 = strongly disagree (12%), 2 (34%), 3 (32%), 4 (16%), 5 (6%).
(iii) the role of schooling in language planning for the Gaelic language:
- *whether 'teaching some children in Gaelic is essential to the future use of Gaelic.* Same response categories as above, 1 = strongly disagree (2%), 2 (11%), 3 (16%), 4 (56%), 5 = strongly agree (15%); and
- *who, if anyone, should have the main responsibility for whether Gaelic is used in Scotland* – response categories: parents who speak Gaelic (36%), local communities (19%), nursery schools and schools (17.6%), the Government (22%), churches (0.4%), the media (1%), other (2%), none of these (2%). Initial exploration of responses found the parents and communities categories to be negatively associated with the likelihood of choice of Gaelic-medium education and for the schools and Government categories to be positively associated with such a likelihood. For the purposes of analysis, the response categories were thus grouped into: 'parents or communities', 'schools or Government' and 'other'.

3.2. Methods

The main method of analysis was binary logistic regression, which aimed to explain the statistical effect of the dimensions and variables outlined in Section 3.1 on the likelihood of choosing Gaelic-medium education. The analysis presents the statistical effects of variables within each individual dimension (Section 4.1) to provide evidence relating to Research Question 1, before considering the statistical effects of variables when all five dimensions are entered in a single statistical model (Section 4.2), to address Research Question 2. We also report summary measures which assess how well the models predict the dependent variable. The tables show the Type II deviance associated with each independent variable, which is defined to be the unique contribution which that variable makes to explaining the dependent variable, conditional on the other variables in the model (Fox & Weisberg, 2011, pp. 238–239). Type II tests of deviance are approximately equivalent to the Wald test of statistical significance for each variable. All modelling was done in the statistical computing environment R and did not use weights. In the tables which follow, categorical explanatory variables measure the statistical effect on the dependent variable by comparison with the specified reference category. For continuous variables, the statistical effect on the dependent variable is measured in relation to a one-unit increase in the value of the explanatory variable.

4. Results

4.1. Research Question 1: when each dimension is modelled individually, which variables are associated with the likelihood of choice of Gaelic-medium education?

4.1.1. Dimension 1: demographic factors
Table 2 shows the relationship between the three demographic variables from Dimension 1 and the dependent variable of likelihood of choice of Gaelic-medium education. The

SUPPORT, TRANSMISSION, EDUCATION AND TARGET VARIETIES

Table 2. Demographic factors and the likelihood of choice of Gaelic-medium education [GME] (negative coefficient meaning lower likelihood of choice of GME than in reference categories).

Explanatory variable (and reference category)		Coeff.	s.e.
Constant		−1.798	.358
Age (ref. 18–24)	25–34	.351	.347
	35–44	.220	.336
	45–54	.066	.338
	55–64	.260	.335
	65+	−.023	.339
Highest educational qualification (ref. 'Tertiary education')	Upper secondary school qualifications	.142	.206
	Middle secondary school qualifications	.133	.202
	None	.668**	.223
Scottish Index of Multiple Deprivation (ref. Group 5, 20% *least deprived* areas in Scotland)	Group 4	.102	.259
	Group 3	.718**	.244
	Group 2	.701**	.244
	Group 1 (20% *most deprived* areas)	.942**	.259
Residual deviance		1099.4	
Number of residual degrees of freedom		950	

	Type II deviance	df	p
Age	3.20	5	.67
Highest educational qualification	9.41	3	.02*
Scottish Index of Multiple Deprivation	22.7	4	.00**

Notes: Key for statistical significance levels: **$p < .01$; *.$01 < p < .05$; (*).$05 < p < .10$. Sample size = 963. The entries are regression coefficients ('Coeff.') and their standard errors ('s.e.') in a binary logistic regression of the dichotomous variable recording likelihood or not of sending a child to Gaelic-medium education (for details, see Section 3.1). The explanatory variables are all categorical, and the coefficients show deviations from the reference category indicated.

deviance values at the foot of the table show that the strongest demographic predictor is the level of social deprivation of the local area in which the respondent lives (Type II deviance: 22.7); the regression coefficients in the upper part show that respondents living in any of the three most deprived fifths are more likely, at the 1% significance level, to place a child in Gaelic-medium education than those living in the 20% least deprived areas of Scotland. The second strongest demographic predictor is a respondent's education level (deviance = 9.4). Compared with those educated to degree level, those with no qualifications are more likely (at the 1% significance level) to express a likelihood to choose Gaelic-medium education for their child. Respondents' age does not make an additional independent contribution to the likelihood of choosing Gaelic-medium education within this model (Type II deviance p-value = .67).

4.1.2. Dimension 2: exposure to Gaelic

Table 3 shows the relationship between the three exposure variables from Dimension 2 and the dependent variable. The deviance values show competence in Gaelic to be the strongest predictor of the likelihood of choice (deviance = 19.4), with (from the upper part of the table) respondents who understood some Gaelic being more likely to consider Gaelic-medium education than those who did not understand any Gaelic. This was true at the 5% significance level for those who understood the odd word of Gaelic, and at the 1% significance level for those who understood at least a few simple sentences. The second strongest demographic predictor is 'exposure to Gaelic in childhood' (deviance = 4.60). The more frequently respondents were exposed to Gaelic in childhood, the more likely they are (at the 5% significance level) to choose Gaelic-medium education for a child.

SUPPORT, TRANSMISSION, EDUCATION AND TARGET VARIETIES

Table 3. Exposure factors and the likelihood of choice of Gaelic-medium education (negative coefficient meaning lower likelihood of choice of GME than in reference categories for categorical variables, and lower likelihood with each one-unit increase in the value of the explanatory variable for continuous variables).

Explanatory variable		Coeff.	s.e.
Constant		−1.726	.224
Competence in understanding Gaelic (ref. None)	The odd word	.444*	.176
	More than the odd word	1.728**	.429
Exposure to Gaelic in the last 12 months (scale where 1 = no exposure and 5 = regular exposure)		.199	.122
Exposure to Gaelic in childhood (scale where 1 = no exposure and 6 = daily exposure)		.131*	.061
Residual deviance		1079.8	
Number of residual degrees of freedom		958	
	Type II deviance	df	p
Competence in understanding Gaelic	19.4	2	.00**
Exposure to Gaelic in the last 12 months	2.64	1	.10
Exposure to Gaelic in childhood	4.60	1	.03*

Note: Key for statistical significance levels: **$p < .01$; *.01 $< p < .05$; (*).05 $< p < .10$. Sample size = 963.
The entries are regression coefficients ('Coeff.') and their standard errors ('s.e.') in a binary logistic regression of the dichotomous variable recording likelihood or not of sending a child to Gaelic-medium education (for details, see Section 3.1). The explanatory variables 'Scale of Exposure to Gaelic' and 'Gaelic in childhood' are continuous. The variable representing respondents' Gaelic competence is categorical, and the coefficients show deviations from the reference category of no Gaelic competence.

However, the variable recording the frequency of respondents' recent exposure to Gaelic (in the year prior to interview) was found to have no independent effect on the dependent variable over and above the competence and exposure in childhood variables (Type II deviance p-value = .10).

4.1.3. Dimension 3: national and cultural identity

Table 4 shows all four identity variables from Dimension 3 to make a statistically significant contribution to explaining the dependent variable. The deviance values show the perceived importance of Gaelic to the respondent's own cultural heritage to be the strongest predictor of likelihood of choosing Gaelic-medium education for a child (deviance = 50.8), with the greater the importance a respondent accords to Gaelic in this domain, the greater the likelihood of choice (at the 1% significance level). The same pattern is evident in relation to the second strongest predictor: respondents' perception of the importance of Gaelic to Scotland's cultural heritage (deviance = 22.4, association significant at the 1% level). The variable with the third strongest explanatory power is the respondent's national identity (deviance = 21.2). The table shows that, compared to the reference category of 'Scottish not British', respondents who felt equally Scottish and British were statistically significantly less likely, at the 1% significance level, to express a likelihood to choose Gaelic-medium education. This was also the case, at the 10% significance level, for those who felt 'more British than Scottish'. The fourth explanatory variable in the model – the importance of Gaelic to the cultural heritage of the Highlands and Islands – makes a unique contribution to explaining the likelihood of choice of Gaelic-medium education, but has much lower explanatory power than the other identity variables (deviance = 6.72). The greater the perceived importance of Gaelic in the cultural heritage

SUPPORT, TRANSMISSION, EDUCATION AND TARGET VARIETIES

Table 4. Identity factors and the likelihood of choice of Gaelic-medium education (negative coefficient meaning lower likelihood of choice of GME than in reference categories for categorical variables, and lower likelihood with each one-unit increase in the value of the explanatory variable for continuous variables).

Explanatory variable		Coeff.	s.e.
Constant		−5.702	.650
National identity (ref. Scottish not British)	More Scottish than British	−.177	.214
	Equally Scottish and British	−.891**	.234
	More British than Scottish	−.690(*)	.408
	British not Scottish	−.497	.453
	Other	.292	.412
Importance of Gaelic to one's own cultural heritage		.450**	.064
(1 = not at all important, 5 = very important)			
Importance of Gaelic to cultural heritage of Highlands and Islands		.372*	.148
(1 = not at all important, 5 = very important)			
Importance of Gaelic to cultural heritage of Scotland		.559**	.127
(1 = not at all important, 5 = very important)			
Residual deviance		899.2	
Number of residual degrees of freedom		954	

	Type II deviance	df	p
National identity	21.2	5	.00**
Importance of Gaelic to own cultural heritage	50.8	1	.00**
Importance of Gaelic to cultural heritage of Highlands and Islands	6.72	1	.01**
Importance of Gaelic to cultural heritage of Scotland	22.4	1	.00**

Notes: Key for statistical significance levels: ** $p < .01$; * $.01 < p < .05$; (*) $.05 < p < .10$. Sample size = 963. The entries are regression coefficients ('Coeff.') and their standard errors ('s.e.') in a binary logistic regression of the dichotomous variable recording likelihood or not of sending a child to Gaelic-medium education (for details, see Section 3.1). The explanatory variables 'Importance of Gaelic to (i) one's own cultural heritage, (ii) the cultural heritage of the Highlands and Islands and (iii) the cultural heritage of Scotland are continuous and measured on a scale from 1 = not at all important to 5 = very important. The variable representing respondents' national identity competence is categorical, and the coefficients show deviations from the reference category of 'Scottish not British'.

of the Highlands and Islands, the greater the likelihood of choice, at the 5% significance level.

4.1.4. Dimension 4: views about the future of Gaelic

Table 5 shows the relationship between the four variables from Dimension 4 and the dependent variable. The deviance values show respondents' hopes for the number of Gaelic speakers in 50 years' time to be the strongest predictor of the likelihood of choice of Gaelic-medium education (deviance = 53.1). Compared to those who hope that there will be fewer speakers in 50 years' time than at present, those who hope that there will be more Gaelic speakers are more likely to choose Gaelic-medium education for their child (at the 1% significance level), and those who hope there will be about the same number of Gaelic speakers are more likely to do so at the 5% level. The second strongest predictor of choice relates to respondents' views on encouraging the use of Gaelic in Scotland (deviance = 43.6). Those who believe that the use of Gaelic should be encouraged in areas where it is already spoken are less likely (at the 1% significance level) to choose Gaelic-medium education for their child than those who believe Gaelic should not be encouraged at all. This seemingly surprising finding is explained by an interaction effect (not shown in the table) with the variable that asks for respondents' views on who should have main responsibility for the future use of Gaelic in Scotland (variable 6 within the 'Gaelic in education' dimension, Section 3.1).[7] The interaction effect showed that people who believe that the use of Gaelic should be encouraged

SUPPORT, TRANSMISSION, EDUCATION AND TARGET VARIETIES

Table 5. Gaelic in the future factors and the likelihood of choice of Gaelic-medium education (negative coefficient meaning lower likelihood of choice of GME than in reference categories).

Explanatory variable (and reference category)		Coeff.	s.e.
Constant		−3.946	.735
Views on encouraging the use of Gaelic in Scotland (ref. 'should not be encouraged at all')	Should be encouraged in areas where it is already spoken	−.890**	.328
	Should be encouraged everywhere in Scotland	.338	.326
Expectations for the number of Gaelic speakers in 50 years' time (ref. 'fewer people than now')	About the same number of people as now	.210	.201
	More people than now	.673**	.228
Hopes for the number of Gaelic speakers in 50 years' time (ref. 'fewer people than now')	About the same number of people as now	1.691*	.760
	More people than now	2.934**	.753
Views on current levels of public spending on Gaelic (ref. 'too much money')	About the right about of money	.864**	.243
	Too little money	1.129**	.278
Residual deviance		842.4	
Number of residual degrees of freedom		954	

	Type II deviance	df	p
Views on encouraging the use of Gaelic in Scotland	43.6	2	.00**
Expectations for the number of Gaelic speakers in 50 years' time	8.74	2	.01**
Hopes for the number of Gaelic speakers in 50 years' time	53.1	2	.00**
Views on current levels of public spending on Gaelic	18.8	2	.00**

Notes: Key for statistical significance levels: **$p < .01$; *.01 $< p < .05$; (*).05 $< p < .10$. Sample size = 963.
The entries are regression coefficients ('Coeff.') and their standard errors ('s.e.') in a binary logistic regression of the dichotomous variable recording likelihood or not of sending a child to Gaelic-medium education (for details, see Section 3.1). The explanatory variables are all categorical, and the coefficients show deviations from the reference category indicated.

only in areas in which it is already spoken typically perceive such work to be the responsibility of local communities and Gaelic speakers, rather than being the responsibility of schools, the government or other agencies. Such respondents seem to be attributing responsibility for the future of Gaelic to its speakers – not to schools, not to government, and not to themselves in the sense of placing a child in Gaelic-medium education. The variable with the third strongest explanatory power within the 'future of Gaelic' dimension is the respondent's view on the current levels of public spending on Gaelic (deviance = 18.8). Compared to those who feel that too much money is being spent on Gaelic, those who believe that about the right amount, or too little, is being spent, are more likely (at the 1% significance level) to express an interest in Gaelic-medium education. The explanatory power of the fourth variable, expectations of the number of Gaelic speakers in 50 years' time, is smaller (deviance = 8.74). Compared to those who expect there to be fewer Gaelic speakers in 50 years' time, those who expect there to be more Gaelic speakers are more likely to choose Gaelic-medium education (at the 1% significance level).

4.1.5. Dimension 5: views on Gaelic in education

Table 6 shows the relationship between the six variables from Dimension 5 and the dependent variable. The deviance values in the lower part of the table show that all six variables make a unique contribution to explaining the likelihood of choice of Gaelic-medium education, but that they differ in their explanatory power. For the purposes of parsimony, the results of Table 6 will be presented in the variable pairs of Gaelic as pedagogy (variables 1 and 2), views about the usefulness of learning Gaelic (variables 3 and 4) and views about education in language planning for Gaelic (variables 5 and 6). Separate analyses showed

SUPPORT, TRANSMISSION, EDUCATION AND TARGET VARIETIES

Table 6. Gaelic in education factors and the likelihood of choice of Gaelic-medium education (negative coefficient meaning lower likelihood of choice of GME than in reference categories for categorical variables, and lower likelihood with each one-unit increase in the value of the explanatory variable for continuous variables).

Explanatory variable		Coeff.	s.e.
Constant		−2.010	.761
Gaelic-medium pupils do better at school than English-medium pupils (1 = strongly disagree, 5 = strongly agree)		.739**	.133
Teaching children in Gaelic is bad because it separates them from children taught in English (1 = strongly disagree, 5 = strongly agree)		−.395**	.100
Learning languages such as French is more useful than learning Gaelic (1 = strongly disagree, 5 = strongly agree)		−.456**	.086
Learning the Gaelic language is pointless in the twenty-first century (1 = strongly disagree, 5 = strongly agree)		−.452**	.102
Teaching some children in Gaelic is essential to the future use of Gaelic (1 = strongly disagree, 5 = strongly agree)		.575**	.125
View on who should have the main responsibility for whether Gaelic is used in Scotland (ref. 'Gaelic-speaking parents' or 'communities')	Schools or government	.876**	.176
	Other	.934*	.418
Residual deviance		840.9	
Number of residual degrees of freedom		955	

	Type II deviance	df	p
Gaelic-medium pupils do better at school than English-medium pupils	34.5	1	.00**
Teaching children in Gaelic is bad because it separates them from children taught in English	16.6	1	.00**
Learning languages such as French is more useful than learning Gaelic	29.3	1	.00**
Learning the Gaelic language is pointless in the twenty-first century	20.7	1	.00**
Teaching some children in Gaelic is essential to the future use of Gaelic	23.3	1	.00**
View on who should have the main responsibility for whether Gaelic is used in Scotland	26.7	2	.00**

Notes: Key for statistical significance levels: **$p < .01$; *.$01 < p < .05$; (*).$05 < p < .10$. Sample size = 963.
The entries are regression coefficients ('Coeff.') and their standard errors ('s.e.') in a binary logistic regression of the dichotomous variable recording likelihood or not of sending a child to Gaelic-medium education (for details, see Section 3.1). The first five explanatory variables in the table are continuous and measured on a scale from 1 = strongly disagree to 5 = strongly agree. The variable representing respondents' view about who should have the main responsibility for whether Gaelic is used in Scotland is categorical, and the coefficients show deviations from the combined reference category of 'parents' and 'communities'. The 'other' category includes people who felt that individuals, the media, the church or other institutions were responsible for whether Gaelic is used in Scotland.

the deviance value of each *pair* of variables, that is to say, the unique contribution of the pair of variables to the model, over and above the explanatory power of the other four variables, to be 50.2, 64.7 and 53.5 for the pedagogy, public politics and language planning variable pairs, respectively.

Respondents' views of the value of learning Gaelic ('education as public politics') were the strongest predictors of the likelihood of choice of Gaelic-medium education within this model (deviance = 64.7). The more valuable a respondent felt Gaelic was (indexed by extent of disagreement with the statements 'learning languages such as French is more useful than learning Gaelic' or 'learning the Gaelic language is pointless in the twenty-first century'), the greater the likelihood of choosing Gaelic-medium education (each variable was significant at the 1% significance level). Respondents' views of the role of Gaelic education in Gaelic-language maintenance also made a significant contribution to the explanatory power of the model (deviance = 53.5). Agreement with the proposition that Gaelic-medium education is essential to the future use of Gaelic was positively associated with likelihood of choice at the 1% significance level, as was a belief that institutions (schools or government) rather than individuals (Gaelic-speaking parents or communities) should have the main responsibility for the continued use of Gaelic in Scotland.[8] In terms

SUPPORT, TRANSMISSION, EDUCATION AND TARGET VARIETIES

of Gaelic-medium education as pedagogy (deviance = 50.2), there was a positive association, at the 1% significance level, between agreement with the proposition that Gaelic-medium pupils do better at school than English-medium pupils and likelihood to choose Gaelic-medium education, and a negative association between likelihood of choice and the extent to which respondents felt Gaelic-medium education to be a bad thing, as it separates Gaelic-medium and English-medium pupils.

4.2. Research Question 2: when all five dimensions are modelled together, which dimensions have the strongest independent statistical influence on the likelihood of choice of Gaelic-medium education, and which variables retain statistical significance?

Table 7 shows the relationship between all the explanatory variables (Dimensions 1–5) and the dependent variable. The deviance values in Table 8 are presented by 'dimension' (as detailed in Section 3.1), since one of our interests in this final model is to gauge the relative importance of the different *kinds* of explanatory variable represented by each dimension in predicting the likelihood of choice of Gaelic-medium education. Table 8 shows that although each dimension makes a unique contribution to explaining the likelihood of choice (Dimensions 1, 3, 4 and 5 at the 1% significance level, and Dimension 2 at the 10% level), 'attitudes to Gaelic in education' (Dimension 5, deviance: 50.6) and 'attitudes to the future of Gaelic' (Dimension 4, deviance: 48.0) are the strongest predictors. 'Demographic characteristics' and 'cultural and national identity' have substantial explanatory power in predicting the dependent variable (Dimension 1, deviance = 34.0 and Dimension 3, deviance = 26.2, respectively), whilst 'exposure to Gaelic' has low explanatory power (Dimension 2, deviance = 8.92).

Table 9 presents the deviance values of each explanatory variable, and shows that 11 of the 18 variables that made statistically significant individual contributions to predicting the dependent variable when the dimensions were modelled individually (Tables 2–6) continue to do so when all five dimensions are modelled together. Five variables within 'attitudes to Gaelic in education' retain statistical significance in the final model, as do two within 'attitudes to the future of Gaelic', two within 'cultural and national identity' and one within each of 'demographic characteristics' and 'exposure to Gaelic'. The patterns of the associations of these variables replicate those detailed in Section 4.1, and thus the present discussion will focus on the levels of statistical significance of the co-efficients within these variables in relation to the likelihood of choice of Gaelic-medium education (Table 7).

Within the 'Gaelic in education' dimension, the two pedagogy variables ('Gaelic-medium pupils do better at school than English-medium pupils' and 'teaching some children in Gaelic is a bad thing because it separates them from children taught in English') retained their 1% statistical significance in the final model, as did the education as language planning variable which asked respondents who should have the principal responsibility for whether Gaelic is used in Scotland. The education as language planning variable which recorded respondents' perceptions of the importance of teaching some children in Gaelic to the future use of Gaelic, retained significance in the final model, but this reduced from 1% to 5%. With regard to education as public politics, disagreement with the statement that learning languages such as French is more useful than learning

SUPPORT, TRANSMISSION, EDUCATION AND TARGET VARIETIES

Table 7. Factors in the likelihood of choice of Gaelic-medium education (negative coefficient meaning lower likelihood of choice of GME than in reference categories for categorical variables, and lower likelihood with each one-unit increase in the value of the explanatory variable for continuous variables).

Dimension	Explanatory variable		Coeff.	s.e.
	Constant		−7.078	1.525
1. Demographic factors	Age (ref. 18–24)	25–34	.248	.458
		35–44	.088	.437
		45–54	−.103	.441
		55–64	.647	.449
		65+	.455	.455
	Highest educational qualification (ref. 'Tertiary education')	Upper secondary school qualifications	.644*	.277
		Middle secondary school qualifications	.514(*)	.272
		None	.942**	.311
	Scottish Index of Multiple Deprivation (ref. Group 5, 20% least deprived areas in Scotland)	Group 4	−.155	.336
		Group 3	.575(*)	.319
		Group 2	.204	.326
		Group 1 (20% *most deprived* areas)	.416	.343
2. Exposure to Gaelic	Competence in understanding Gaelic (ref. None)	The odd word	.057	.237
		More than the odd word (from 'a few simple sentences' to 'all conversations')	1.398*	.589
	Exposure to Gaelic in the last 12 months (scale where 1 = no exposure and 5 = regular exposure)		−.146	.165
	Exposure to Gaelic in childhood (scale where 1 = no exposure and 6 = daily exposure)		.088	.083
3. National and cultural identity	National identity (ref. Scottish not British)	More Scottish than British	−.077	.256
		Equally Scottish and British	−.663*	.276
		More British than Scottish	−.324	.482
		British not Scottish	−.153	.570
		Other	.869	.535
	Importance of Gaelic to one's own cultural heritage (1 = not at all important, 5 = very important)		.162*	.082
	Importance of Gaelic to cultural heritage of Highlands and Islands (1 = not at all important, 5 = very important)		.166	.172
	Importance of Gaelic to cultural heritage of Scotland (1 = not at all important, 5 = very important)		.210	.157
4. Gaelic in the future	Views on encouraging the use of Gaelic in Scotland (ref. 'should not be encouraged at all')	Should be encouraged in areas where it is already spoken	−.748(*)	.416
		Should be encouraged everywhere in Scotland	.115	.406
	Expectations for the number of Gaelic speakers in 50 years' time (ref. 'fewer people than now')	About the same number of people as now	.219	.233
		More people than now	.260	.275
	Hopes for the number of Gaelic speakers in 50 years' time (ref. 'fewer people than now')	About the same number of people as now	1.490	.944
		More people than now	2.338*	.946
	Views on current levels of public spending on Gaelic (ref. 'too much money')	About the right about of money	.281	.330
		Too little money	.349	.330

(Continued)

SUPPORT, TRANSMISSION, EDUCATION AND TARGET VARIETIES

Table 7. Continued.

Dimension	Explanatory variable		Coeff.	s.e.
5. Gaelic in education	Gaelic-medium pupils do better at school than English-medium pupils (1 = strongly disagree, 5 = strongly agree)		.618**	.155
	Teaching children in Gaelic is bad because it separates them from children taught in English (1 = strongly disagree, 5 = strongly agree)		−.366**	.113
	Learning languages such as French is more useful than learning Gaelic (1 = strongly disagree, 5 = strongly agree)		−.183(*)	.104
	Learning the Gaelic language is pointless in the twenty-first century (1 = strongly disagree, 5 = strongly agree)		−.104	.123
	Teaching some children in Gaelic is essential to the future use of Gaelic (1 = strongly disagree, 5 = strongly agree)		.304*	.152
	View on who should have the main responsibility for whether Gaelic is used in Scotland (ref. 'parents' or 'communities')	Schools or government	.548**	.210
		Other	.383	.475
	Residual deviance		687.8	
	Number of residual degrees of freedom		923	

Notes: Key for statistical significance levels: **$p < .01$; *.01 $< p < .05$; (*).05 $< p < .10$. Sample size = 963.
The entries are regression coefficients ('Coeff.') and their standard errors ('s.e.') in a binary logistic regression of the dichotomous variable recording likelihood or not of sending a child to Gaelic-medium education (for details, see Section 3.1). See notes to Tables 3–6 for specification of explanatory variables.

Table 8. Analysis of Type II deviance corresponding to Table 7 (by dimension).

	Type II deviance	df	p
Dimension			
1. Demographic	34.0**	12	<.001
2. Exposure to Gaelic	8.92***	4	.06
3. Identity	26.2**	8	.001
4. Gaelic in the future	48.0**	8	<.001
5. Gaelic in education	50.6**	7	<.001

Note: Key for statistical significance levels: **$p < .01$; *.01 $< p < .05$; (*).05 $< p < .10$. Sample size = 963.

Gaelic retained an association with the likelihood of choice, but at a reduced significance level (10% rather than 1%).

Within the 'future of Gaelic' dimension, the variables 'hopes for the number of Gaelic speakers in 50 years' time' and 'views of encouraging the use of Gaelic in Scotland' continued to have a statistical association with the dependent variable in the final model, but at reduced levels of significance as compared to the model which contained only this dimension (Table 5). In the full model (Table 7), there is now only a statistical association between those who wish there to be *more* people speaking Gaelic in 50 years' time and likelihood of choice of Gaelic-medium education, with this association now at the 5% significance level. The negative association with likelihood of choice of the belief that Gaelic should be encouraged only in areas in which it is already spoken (see Section 4.1) is now significant at the 10%, rather than the 1% level.

Within 'cultural and national identity', the variable recording the importance of Gaelic to the respondent's cultural heritage retained its positive association with the dependent variable (but now at the 5% significance level), whilst, for national identity, the final model replicated the finding that those who identify as Scottish not British are more

SUPPORT, TRANSMISSION, EDUCATION AND TARGET VARIETIES

Table 9. Analysis of Type II deviance corresponding to Table 7 by variable.

Dimension	Variable	Type II deviance	df	p
1. Demographic factors	Age	6.84	5	.23
	Highest educational qualification	11.3*	3	.01
	Scottish Index of Multiple Deprivation	7.34	4	.12
2. Exposure to Gaelic	Competence in understanding Gaelic	6.29*	2	.04
	Exposure to Gaelic in the last 12 months	0.784	1	.38
	Exposure to Gaelic in childhood	1.12	1	.29
3. National and cultural identity	National identity	14.0*	5	.02
	Importance of Gaelic to respondent's cultural heritage	3.92*	1	.05
	Importance of Gaelic to cultural heritage of Highlands and Islands	0.956	1	.33
	Importance of Gaelic to cultural heritage of Scotland	1.83	1	.18
4. Gaelic in the future	Views on encouraging the use of Gaelic in Scotland	15.0**	2	.00
	Expectations for the number of Gaelic speakers in 50 years' time	1.29	2	.52
	Hopes for the number of Gaelic speakers in 50 years' time	16.9**	2	.00
	Views on current levels of public spending on Gaelic	1.27	2	.53
5. Gaelic in education	Gaelic-medium pupils do better at school than English-medium pupils	17.1**	1	.00
	Teaching children in Gaelic is bad because it separates them from children taught in English	11.0**	1	.00
	Learning languages such as French is more useful than learning Gaelic	3.07(*)	1	.08
	Learning the Gaelic language is pointless in the twenty-first century	0.712	1	.40
	Teaching some children in Gaelic is essential to the future use of Gaelic	4.10*	1	.04
	View on who should have the main responsibility for whether Gaelic is used in Scotland	6.80*	2	.03

Note: Key for statistical significance levels: **$p < .01$; *$.01 < p < .05$; (*)$.05 < p < .10$. Sample size = 963.

likely to choose Gaelic-medium education than those who identify as 'equally Scottish and British', but the significance of the association has reduced to 5% in the final model. In relation to 'demographic characteristics', the final model shows an increase in the statistical association of the 'highest educational qualification' variable with likelihood of choice of Gaelic-medium education. In addition to the replication of the finding that those with no qualifications are statistically significantly more likely to choose Gaelic-medium education than those with tertiary-level qualifications (at the 1% significance level), the final model suggests that those with middle secondary school or upper secondary school qualifications are also more likely to so (at the 10% and 5% significance levels, respectively). This finding is explored in Section 5. Finally, within the 'exposure to Gaelic' dimension, competence in Gaelic remains significantly positively associated with the likelihood of choice of Gaelic-medium education in the final model, but now only in relation to those who understand at least a few simple sentences, and now at the 5% significance level. The significance of 11 individual variables across the five dimensions in the final model suggests that multiple rationales pertain to the choice of Gaelic-medium education, a finding that concords with all previous research cited in relation to the Scottish, Welsh and Irish contexts in Section 1.

5. Discussion

5.1. Research Question 1

Research Question 1 asked which variables are statistically associated with the likelihood of choice of Gaelic-medium education when each dimension is modelled individually.

Section 4.1 found 18 variables to be so associated (see Type II deviance p-values, Tables 2–6), and described the key patterns pertaining to these variables. The value of such simple statistics is that it enables comparison with previous research on choice of Gaelic-medium education, whose methods often equate to a univariate approach. That is to say, the previous research typically notes the factors which are associated with the choice of Gaelic-medium education individually, without considering statistically the relative influence of each factor when multiple explanations are involved (Johnstone et al., 1999; MacNeil, 1993; O'Hanlon, 2015; O'Hanlon et al., 2010).[9]

The findings of the present research largely concorded with those of the previous research, with 10 of the 12 variables which were comparable with these previous studies replicating their findings. These were the association with the likelihood of choice of Gaelic-medium education of: the two variables within the 'exposure dimension' (competence in Gaelic, exposure in childhood) (Johnstone et al., 1999; MacNeil, 1993; O'Hanlon et al., 2010; Stockdale et al., 2003), the four variables within the 'national and cultural identity' dimension (national identity, and perceptions of the importance of Gaelic to the cultural identity of the respondent, of the Highlands and Islands, and of Scotland) (Johnstone et al., 1999; MacNeil, 1993; O'Hanlon, 2015; O'Hanlon et al., 2010), the two pedagogy variables within the 'Gaelic and education' dimension (outcomes of Gaelic-medium, pedagogical context) (Johnstone et al., 1999; MacNeil, 1993; O'Hanlon et al., 2010; Stockdale et al., 2003), and the two language planning variables within the 'Gaelic and education' dimension, which reflect the role of education in the maintenance of Gaelic (MacNeil, 1993; O'Hanlon et al., 2010). The findings of the present research which did not concord with previous findings were that those with no qualifications are more likely than those with a tertiary-level educational qualification to say that they would choose Gaelic-medium education for their child, as were those living in the most deprived areas of Scotland. The finding on education level marks a shift from previous literature, which showed the likelihood of choice of Gaelic-medium education to be associated with parents with tertiary or upper secondary school qualifications (Stockdale et al., 2003). We return to a discussion of education level in relation to choice in Research Question 2 (below).

The findings on likelihood of choice and the Scottish Index of Multiple Deprivation – which indicate that those living in areas that are among the three most deprived fifths of SIMD areas in Scotland are more likely to consider Gaelic-medium education than those living in the 20% least deprived areas – also appear to contradict what is known from other sources about enacted choice, where pupils from the most deprived areas are relatively under-represented in Gaelic-medium education. One possible explanation for the different finding may be inferred from results reported by O'Hanlon et al. (2010), who found the schools that had Gaelic-medium streams generally served pupils that were less socially disadvantaged than the average (within these schools, there was no social distinction between pupils in the Gaelic-medium and the English-medium streams). In 2014–2015, only 1 of the 59 Gaelic-medium primary providers was located in one of the 20% most highly deprived areas of Scotland, as defined by school postcode, and only 9% of Gaelic-medium primary educated pupils lived in one of these areas (Scottish Government, 2016).[10] It could be that our finding here indicates a preference to have better access to Gaelic-medium schooling by socially disadvantaged families who do not live close to a school which provides Gaelic-medium education.[11] Such a broadening of

SUPPORT, TRANSMISSION, EDUCATION AND TARGET VARIETIES

demand would be consistent with patterns of growth in Welsh-medium education and Irish-medium education in Anglicised areas (Bellin et al., 1999; Kavanagh & Hickey, 2013; Thomas, 2013) and would also be consistent with research from English-medium education which showed the stable operation of parental choice after the initial period in the 1980s when choice was more often exercised by socially advantaged parents than by others: in due course, parents from across the social spectrum were able to use placing requests to gain access to their choice of school (Croxford & Paterson, 2006; Gorard & Fitz, 1998; Gorard, Fitz, & Taylor, 2001). Future research would be required to investigate empirically the factors mediating between intended and enacted choice of Gaelic-medium education, in order to identify the factors that enable or restrict access to Gaelic-medium education in Scotland. Such research should consider both community-level factors (such as distance to GME provision, and availability of information on GME), and respondent-level characteristics (such as socio-economic status).

The remaining six variables found to be statistically significantly associated with a likelihood of choice of Gaelic-medium education were variables without precedence in the previous literature. These were: the four variables within the 'Gaelic in the future' dimension and the two on the perceived value of learning Gaelic within the 'Gaelic in education' dimension (Sections 3.1 and 4.1, Dimensions 4 and 5). These variables, which indexed respondents' views on the future of Gaelic, on promoting and supporting Gaelic, and on the usefulness and relevance of learning Gaelic, were included in order that we would have a suite of explanatory variables which would reflect Baker's tripartite framework – of language planning, pedagogy and politics – when modelling the factors associated with the likelihood of choice within one statistical model (to address Research Question 2).

5.2. Research Question 2

Research Question 2 investigated which of the five dimensions had the strongest independent statistical influence on the likelihood of choice of Gaelic-medium education when all five dimensions were modelled together, and which individual variables retained statistical significance within this final model. The use of logistic regression to model the influence of the five dimensions and their 20 constitutive variables on likelihood of choice enabled us to show a more nuanced and complex pattern of results than that found in previous, predominantly univariate, research on the choice of Gaelic-medium education in Scotland. The methodological approach enabled us to evaluate the relative contribution of each dimension to likelihood of choice of Gaelic-medium education, with a key finding being the relative unimportance of the 'exposure to Gaelic' dimension, which indexes both competence in Gaelic and exposure to the language (Table 8). The much higher contribution of the 'national and cultural identity' dimension reflects the importance of the symbolic social role of Gaelic in the likelihood of choice of Gaelic-medium education amongst this representative sample of the Scottish population. Such a finding reflects both the low levels of competence in Gaelic amongst the general population in Scotland (with only 1.7% of the population reporting any skills in Gaelic in the 2011 census), and is an instance of a wider phenomenon in which people's views about the symbolic role of Gaelic are typically more strongly associated with views of public policy for Gaelic than are views about the communicative role of the language (National Records of Scotland, 2015; Paterson & O'Hanlon, 2015).

The methodological approach also enabled us to illustrate the value of simultaneously considering a range of dimensions when investigating the choice of medium of education, as only 11 of the 18 variables found to be statistically significant when each dimension was modelled individually retained significance in the final model which modelled all five dimensions together. The significant variables within the final model were presented by dimension in Section 4.2 to enable comparison with the results of Research Question 1 and with the previous literature.

However, here, the statistically significant results from the final model (Table 7) will be discussed in relation to Baker's (2000) tripartite framework of language planning, pedagogy and politics, as a key aim of the paper is to investigate the extent to which Baker's three contexts for growth of Welsh-medium education underpin potential growth of Gaelic-medium education in Scotland (Section 2.2). Table 9 presents the deviance values of each individual variable which can be associated with Baker's three contexts for growth: planning (two planning variables within 'Gaelic in education' dimension plus the four variables within 'future of Gaelic' dimension), pedagogy (two pedagogy variables within 'Gaelic in education' dimension) and public politics (two politics variables within 'Gaelic in education' dimension plus the four variables within the 'national and cultural identity' dimension). In analysis not shown in the table, when the combined deviance values of each context are calculated within the full model (as shown in Table 7), the Type II deviance associated with each context was: planning $= 76.1$ (11 degrees of freedom, $p < .001$), pedagogy $= 28.0$ (2 degrees of freedom, $p < .001$), and politics $= 36.50$ (10 degrees of freedom, $p < .001$), showing each context to have a significant influence on the likelihood of Gaelic-medium education in the Scottish context.

With regard to bilingual education as language planning, evidence from the two significant planning variables included in the 'Gaelic in education' dimension was supplemented by evidence from the two significant variables within the 'views about the future of Gaelic' dimension. In summary, respondents were more likely to choose Gaelic-medium education if they hoped that the number of Gaelic speakers would increase over the next 50 years, if they felt that Gaelic-medium education was essential to the future of Gaelic in Scotland, and if they felt that institutions (the school or government) were the main stakeholders responsible for the future use of Gaelic in Scotland. The last conclusion here is based on evidence from two interacting variables: the finding that those who explicitly identify institutions (rather than parents and communities) as having the main responsibility for whether Gaelic is used in Scotland are more likely to choose Gaelic-medium education for their child, and the finding that those who believe that Gaelic should be promoted only in areas where it is already spoken (and who, within this survey, typically perceive such work to be the responsibility of parents and local communities) are less likely to choose Gaelic-medium education. Such evidence relates to the debate about the role of education in language revitalisation (for summary, see Ó Laoire & Harris, 2006). In relation to bilingual education as pedagogy, the two pedagogy variables from the 'Gaelic in education' dimension retained strong levels of statistical significance and predictive power in the final model. These findings concord with the priority accorded to immersion education as an academically successful form of education within a culturally inclusive school context in Scotland (Johnstone et al., 1999; MacNeil, 1993; O'Hanlon, 2015; O'Hanlon et al., 2010; Stephen et al., 2010). Finally, with regard to bilingual education as politics, the evidence from the statistically significant variable from the 'Gaelic in education' dimension is supplemented by two significant variables within the 'national and cultural identity' dimension. In the final model, likelihood of choice of Gaelic-medium education was associated with holding a strongly Scottish national identity, with the respondent perceiving the language to be important to their own cultural heritage, and with perceiving Gaelic to be at least as useful as learning French. The association between a personal cultural link to Gaelic and the choice of Gaelic-medium education is well established (Johnstone et al., 1999; MacNeil, 1993; O'Hanlon, 2015; O'Hanlon et al., 2010; Stephen et al., 2010; Stockdale et al., 2003), whilst a link between national identity and choice of Gaelic-medium education has emerged in some, but not all, previous research (O'Hanlon et al., 2010; Stockdale et al., 2003).

In addition to the nine significant variables that can be classified according to Baker's framework, two other variables retained significance in the final model. Respondents were more likely to express a likelihood to choose Gaelic-medium education if they had some Gaelic-language skills (here indexed as the ability to understand at least a few sentences of Gaelic) and if they did not hold a degree level educational qualification. The finding of competence in Gaelic being linked to likelihood of choice of Gaelic-medium education is well established, with some previous literature acknowledging that such competence may be passive understanding resulting from a family heritage of Gaelic-speaking in a previous generation (MacNeil, 1993; O'Hanlon, 2015; O'Hanlon et al., 2010; Stephen et al., 2010). However, the finding that likelihood of choice is associated with those not educated to degree level diverges from that reported in previous research which found there to be a statistically significant association between education to university or upper secondary level and likelihood of choice of Gaelic-medium education (Stockdale et al., 2003). The difference in the findings may relate to differences in the research studies' samples – the Stockdale et al. (2003) study being conducted within three Gaelic-speaking communities in the Highlands and Islands, and the present study being a nationally representative survey. Alternatively, it may reflect a shift over time in the demographic characteristics of parents interested in Gaelic-medium education in the 10 years between the surveys (2002 and 2012, respectively), a period which saw a 96% growth in the number of Gaelic-medium primary pupils in lowland areas, compared with a 5% increase in the Highlands and Islands (here defined as the three council areas of Comhairle nan Eilean Siar, Highland Council and Argyll & Bute Council). In 2002–2003, 71% of the 1928 pupils in Gaelic-medium primary education were educated in the Highlands and Islands, compared with 58% of the 2500 pupils so educated in 2012–2013 (Galloway, 2012; Robertson, 2002). Limitations in the sample size of the present survey (discussed in Section 6) precludes the analysis of the data by regional area, and limitations of Government data (which does not collect information on parental education level in relation to pupil medium of instruction) prevents a comparison of the socio-economic profile of the Gaelic-medium pupil cohort over time. Similar limitations in the availability of data to evidence change in the profile of parents of Celtic-medium pupils over time have been noted in relation to parents of pupils in all-Irish schools in Ireland between 1985 and 2002 (Harris, Forde, Archer, Nic Fhearaile, & O'Gorman, 2006, p. 158), and in relation to parents of Welsh-medium pupils in Wales (Thomas, 2013, p. 51). A hypothesis of both authors is that the increase in provision of Irish-medium and Welsh-medium education in

Anglicised areas has led to the broadening of parental demographic characteristics (such as education level and socio-economic status) over time, and the results of the present study indicate that this warrants further exploration in the Scottish context.

6. Implications and limitations

The paper has provided statistical evidence relating to the factors associated with a likelihood of choice of Gaelic-medium education amongst a representative sample of the adult population in Scotland. In so doing, it has shown the potential demand for Gaelic-medium education in Scotland (at 28%) to be similar to the level of potential demand found in a methodologically similar survey of 2000 adults in the Republic of Ireland and Northern Ireland conducted in 2000, in which 23% of those surveyed in the Republic, and 21% of Catholics surveyed in the North said that they would send their children to an Irish-medium primary school if it was located near their home (Ó Riagáin, 2007). The findings can also be considered alongside the actual choice of Welsh-medium primary education in Wales (24% in 2014–2015), a context in which Celtic-medium education is available in every local authority (Welsh Government, 2015). The paper has shown Baker's tripartite explanatory framework for the growth of bilingual education in Wales – bilingual education as language planning, as pedagogy and as politics – also to be valuable in explaining potential future growth of Gaelic-medium education. The specific findings of the research may help to inform future language policy and planning in Scotland and may also be useful in cross-national comparisons, particularly with studies which adopt a similar theoretical and methodological approach to investigating the potential demand for bilingual education in lesser-used languages. For example, the findings of the present research could be compared with those of the 2013 *Irish Language Survey*, which contained a similar question about likelihood of choice of Irish-medium primary education for a child if it was locally available (Darmody & Daly, 2015).

However, the present study does have limitations. The first is that the sample size is not large enough to enable the comparative analysis of variables associated with a likelihood of choice of Gaelic-medium education at sub-national levels, for example, a comparison between the most densely Gaelic-speaking areas of the Highlands & Islands and the Lowlands, or between individual education authorities. The second pertains to the use of large-scale quantitative survey data. Although such data are useful for identifying demographic and attitudinal characteristics associated with the likelihood of choice of Gaelic-medium education, a full understanding of the factors and contexts which would facilitate, or which would restrict, the 'enactment' of such 'behavioural intentions' (Fishbein & Ajzen, 1975) would require further in-depth qualitative work. A large-scale qualitative study – which enabled such sub-national comparisons and which investigated parental reasons both for choosing, and for not choosing, Gaelic-medium education – is thus recommended. Following Hickey (1999) and Harris et al. (2006), we would recommend that all future research on the choice of bilingual education include key variables on parental education, socio-economic status and language competence (at parental, family and community levels), and additionally recommend that researchers consider replicating key questions, methodological features or analytic categories from previous research on choice in the UK and internationally. Such measures would better facilitate new strands

SUPPORT, TRANSMISSION, EDUCATION AND TARGET VARIETIES

of work, for example, the analysis of choice of immersion education by social class, which Makropoulos (2007) argues to warrant international attention, and would better enable future longitudinal and cross-national comparisons of reasons for parental choice of bilingual education.

Notes

1. The importance of Gaelic education to the maintenance of Gaelic in Scotland is underlined by 2011 census figures, which show levels of inter-generational transmission of Gaelic to be low. Only 0.4% of 0–2 year olds were reported to have any Gaelic-language skills, compared to a national incidence across age groups of 1.7% (NRS, 2015, p. 11).
2. The analysis presented in Section 4 was also conducted using the dichotomy 'very likely' to choose Gaelic-medium education and 'other responses' (consisting of the categories 'fairly likely', 'not very likely' and 'not at all likely'). The pattern of results was the same, with no coefficient that was significant in one analysis changing direction (from negative to positive, or vice versa) in the other analysis. The analysis based on the 'very likely' and 'other responses' dichotomy is available from the authors on request.
3. In the appendix, statistical significance is assessed at the 10% level.
4. The Scottish Index of Multiple Deprivation uses 37 indicators in the seven domains of Current income, Employment, Health, Education skills and training, Geographic access to services, Housing, and Crime to measure the level of deprivation across Scotland by data-zone (a small geographic area with 500–1000 residents).
5. The Highlands and Islands are the areas of Scotland with the highest density of Gaelic speakers. All civil parishes (small areas of Scotland which originally represented a church parish) with 5% or more of the population reporting themselves to be Gaelic speakers exist within the Highlands and Islands (in the North-West of Scotland) (NRS, 2015, p. 31).
6. The relationship of variables within Dimensions 1–4 to Baker's (2000) three contexts – of education as pedagogy, language planning, and politics – will be discussed in Section 5.
7. That is to say, inserting the interactive effect removed the statistical significance associated with the original variable.
8. The 'other' category within this variable is small (53 respondents) and thus the evidence relating to it is not reliable.
9. As noted earlier, the methodological exception here is Stockdale et al. (2003).
10. In the school year 2014–2015 the SIMD distribution of Gaelic-medium primary pupils by home postcode was: 9% (highest deprivation quintile), 24%, 36%, 19%, 11% (lowest deprivation quintile) [$n = 2901$]. The distribution in English-medium education was: 23% (highest deprivation quintile), 19%, 19%, 20%, 18% [$n = 373,794$] (Scottish Government, 2016).
11. The appendix shows that household income and social class were also associated with the dependent variable: with greater social disadvantage associated with greater likelihood of choice of Gaelic-medium education.

Funding

The research was supported by the UK Economic and Social Research Council under grant [ES/J003352/1]; by the Scottish Government; Bòrd na Gàidhlig; and Soillse.

ORCiD

Fiona O'Hanlon ⓘ http://orcid.org/0000-0002-8387-3303

References

Ajzen, I. (1991). The theory of planned behavior. *Organizational Behavior and Human Decision Processes, 50*, 179–211. doi:10.1016/0749-5978(91)90020-T

Baker, C. (2000). Three perspectives on bilingual education policy in Wales: Bilingual education as language planning, as pedagogy and as politics. In R. Daugherty, R. Phillips, & G. Rees (Eds.), *Education policy making in Wales: Explorations in devolved governance* (pp. 102–123). Cardiff: University of Wales Press.

Baker, C. (2011). *Foundations of bilingual education and bilingualism* (5th ed.). Clevedon: Multilingual Matters.

Bamford, K., & Mizokawa, D. (1991). Additive bilingual (immersion) education: Cognitive and language development. *Language Learning, 41*, 413–429. doi:10.1111/j.1467-1770.1991.tb00612.x

Bellin, W., Farrell, S., Higgs, G., & White, S. (1999). The social context of Welsh-medium bilingual education in anglicised areas. *Journal of Sociolinguistics, 3*, 173–193. doi:10.1111/1467-9481.00071

Bird, B. (1993). Attitudes to Gaelic: Young adults in the Western Isles. In K. MacKinnon (Ed.), *FASGNAG II: Second conference on research and studies on the maintenance of Gaelic* (pp. 1–7). Sleat: Sabhal Mòr Ostaig.

Bush, E., Atkinson, P., & Read, M. (1981). *A minority choice: Welsh-medium education in an Anglicised area - parents' characteristics and motives*. Cardiff: University College of Cardiff.

Cole, A., & Williams, C. (2004). Institutions, identities and lesser-used languages in Wales and Brittany. *Regional and Federal Studies, 14*, 554–579. doi:10.1080/1359756042000315487

Cooper, R. (1989). *Language planning and social change*. Cambridge: Cambridge University Press.

Croxford, L., & Paterson, L. (2006). Trends in social class segregation between schools in England, Wales and Scotland since 1984. *Research Papers in Education, 21*, 381–406. doi:10.1080/02671520600942388

Darmody, M., & Daly, T. (2015). *Attitudes towards the Irish language on the island of Ireland*. Dublin: Economic and Social Research Institute.

Fishbein, M., & Ajzen, I. (1975). *Belief, attitude, intention and behaviour: An introduction to theory and research*. Reading: Addison-Wesley. Retrieved from http://people.umass.edu/aizen/f&a1975.html

Fox, J., & Weisberg, S. (2011). *An R companion to applied regression*. London: Sage.

Galloway, J. (2012). *Gaelic education data. 2012–13*. Inverness: Bòrd na Gàidhlig.

Galloway, J. (2015). *Gaelic education data. 2014–15*. Inverness: Bòrd na Gàidhlig. Retrieved from http://www.gaidhlig.org.uk/bord/wp-content/uploads/sites/2/Dàta-Foghlaim-AM-FOLLAIS-2014-15-egn-2-RELEASED-Education-Data.pdf

Genesee, F. (1983). An invited article: Bilingual education of majority-language children: The immersion experiments in review. *Applied Psycholinguistics, 4*, 1–46. doi:10.1017/S0142716400001739

Gorard, S., & Fitz, J. (1998). The more things change … the missing impact of marketization?. *British Journal of Sociology of Education, 19*, 365–376. http://www.jstor.org/stable/1393241

Gorard, S., Fitz, J., & Taylor, C. (2001). School choice impacts: What do we know? *Educational Researcher, October, 30*, 18–23. doi:10.3102/0013189X030007018

Harris, J., Forde, P., Archer, P., Nic Fhearaile, S., & O'Gorman, M. (2006). *Irish in primary schools: Long-term national trends in achievement*. Dublin: Stationery Office.

Hickey, T. (1999). Parents and early immersion: Reciprocity between home and immersion pre-school. *International Journal of Bilingual Education and Bilingualism, 2*, 94–113.

Hodges, R. S. (2012). Welsh-medium education and parental incentives – The case of the Rhymni Valley, Caerffili. *International Journal of Bilingual Education and Bilingualism, 15*, 355–373. doi:10.1080/13670050.2011.636796

Johnstone, R., Harlen, W., MacNeil, M., Stradling, R., & Thorpe, G. (1999). *The attainments of pupils receiving Gaelic medium education in Scotland*. Stirling: Scottish Centre for Information on Language Teaching.

Kavanagh, L. (2013). *A mixed methods investigation of parental involvement in Irish immersion primary education: Integrating multiple perspectives* (Unpublished PhD Thesis). University College Dublin. Retrieved from http://www.cogg.ie/wp-content/uploads/A-Mixed-Methods-Investigation-of-Parental-Involvement-in-Irish-Immersion-Primary-Education.pdf

SUPPORT, TRANSMISSION, EDUCATION AND TARGET VARIETIES

Kavanagh, L., & Hickey, T. (2013). 'You're looking at this different language and it freezes you out straight away': Identifying challenges to parental involvement among immersion parents. *Language and Education, 27*, 432–450.

MacKinnon, K. (1981). *Scottish opinion on Gaelic: A report on a national attitude survey for An Comunn Gaidhealach*. Hatfield: Hatfield Polytechnic.

MacKinnon, K. (1995). *Identity, attitudes and support for Gaelic policies: Gaelic speakers in the Euromosaic survey 1994–95*. Retrieved from:http://www.sgrud.org.uk/anfy/gaelic_articles/euromosiac_identity_belf.htm

MacLeod, D. J. (2003). An historical overview. In M. Nicolson & M. MacIver (Eds.), *Gaelic medium education* (pp. 1–14). Edinburgh: Dunedin Academic Press.

MacNeil, M. M. (1993). *Parental experience of Gaelic-medium schooling*. Sleat: Lèirsinn.

Maguire, G. (1991). *Our own language: An Irish initiative*. Clevedon: Multilingual Matters.

Makropoulos, J. (2007). Class dynamics in the selection of Early French Immersion Programs in Canada. *Education and Society, 25*(3), 35–50.

Market Research UK. (2003). *Attitudes to the Gaelic language*. Glasgow: Market Research United Kingdom.

Mas-Moury Mack, V. (2013). *Language attitudes of parents in Irish-medium primary schools in County Dublin* (Unpublished PhD thesis). Université Michel de Montaigne Bordeaux. Retrieved from https://tel.archives-ouvertes.fr/tel-01124117/document

National Records of Scotland (2015). *Scotland's census 2011: Gaelic report (part 1)*. Edinburgh: National Records of Scotland. Retrieved from National Records of Scotland website http://www.scotlandscensus.gov.uk/documents/analytical_reports/Report_%20part_1.pdf

Ó Donnagáin, E. (1995). *The development of all-Irish primary schools and parental attitudes towards them* (Unpublished MA thesis). National University of Ireland, Maynooth.

O'Hanlon, F. (2015). Choice of Scottish Gaelic-medium and Welsh-medium education at the primary and secondary school stages: Parent and pupil perspectives. *International Journal of Bilingual Education and Bilingualism, 18*, 242–259. doi:10.1080/13670050.2014.923374

O'Hanlon, F., McLeod, W., & Paterson, L. (2010). *Gaelic-medium education in Scotland: Choice and attainment at the primary and early secondary school stages*. Edinburgh: The University of Edinburgh. Retrieved from http://www.gaidhlig.org.uk/bord/wp-content/uploads/sites/2/CR09-05-GME-Choice-and-Attainment-2010-English1.pdf

Ó Laoire, M., & Harris, J. (2006). *Language and Literacy in Irish-medium primary schools: Review of literature*. Dublin: National Council for Curriculum and Assessment. http://www.ncca.ie/uploadedfiles/primary/lang%20lit%20english.pdf

Ó Riagáin, P. (1997). *Language policy and social reproduction: Ireland 1893–1993*. Oxford: Clarendon.

Ó Riagáin, P. (2007). Relationships between attitudes to Irish, social class, religion and national identity in the Republic of Ireland and Northern Ireland. *International Journal of Bilingual Education and Bilingualism, 10*, 369–393. doi:10.2167/beb450.0

Ó Riagáin, P., & Ó Glasáin, M. (1979). *All-Irish schools in the Dublin area: Report of a sociological and spatial study of all-Irish-medium schools in the greater Dublin area, with special reference to their impact on home and social network use of Irish*. Dublin: Institiúid Teangeolaíochta Éireann.

Packer, A., & Campbell, C. (1997). *The reasons for parental choice of Welsh-medium education: A qualitative study of parental attitudes, undertaken in the catchment area of a Welsh-medium primary school, in an Anglicized area*. Aberystwyth: Undeb Cenedlaethol Athrawon Cymru.

Paterson, L., & O'Hanlon, F. (2015). Public views of minority languages as communication or symbol: The case of Gaelic in Scotland. *Journal of Multilingual and Multicultural Development, 36*, 555–570. doi:10.1080/01434632.2014.972959

Ricciardelli, L. A. (1992). Bilingualism and cognitive development in relation to threshold theory. *Journal of Psycholinguistic Research, 21*, 301–316. Retrieved from http://link.springer.com/

Robertson, B. (2002). *Gaelic-medium education in primary schools: Pupil numbers 2002–03*. Glasgow: University of Strathclyde.

ScotCen Social Research (2013a). *Scottish social attitudes survey 2012* [Data Set] (2nd ed.). Colchester: UK Data Archive [distributor]. http://dx.doi.org/10.5255/UKDA-SN-7338-2

ScotCen Social Research (2013b). *Scottish social attitudes survey 2012: User guide*. Edinburgh: ScotCen Social Research. Retrieved from http://dx.doi.org/10.5255/UKDA-SN-7338-2

Scottish Government. (2009). *Scottish index of multiple deprivation: 2009 general report*. Edinburgh: Scottish Government. Retrieved from http://www.gov.scot/Publications/2009/10/28104046/0

Scottish Government. (2011). *Attitudes towards the Gaelic language*. Edinburgh: Scottish Government. Retrieved from http://www.gov.scot/Publications/2011/08/04160631/0

Scottish Government. (2015a). *Education (Scotland) Bill 2015: Business and regulatory impact assessment*. Edinburgh: Scottish Government. Retrieved from http://www.gov.scot/Publications/2015/03/1634/1

Scottish Government. (2015b). *The Education (Scotland) Bill 2015: Information for parents*. Edinburgh: Scottish Government. Retrieved from http://www.gov.scot/Resource/0047/00473658.pdf

Scottish Government. (2016). 'Gaelic-medium education by SIMD quintile'. Data provided by Scottish Government, 08.04.16.

Scottish Parliament. (2016). *Education (Scotland) Act*. Edinburgh: Scottish Parliament. Retrieved from http://www.legislation.gov.uk/asp/2016/8/introduction/enacted

Stephen, C., McPake, J., McLeod, W., Pollock, I., & Carroll, T. (2010). *Review of Gaelic-medium early education and childcare*. Edinburgh: Scottish Government Social Research.

Stockdale, A., MacGregor, B., & Munro, G. (2003). *Migration, Gaelic-medium education and language use*. Sleat: National Centre for Migration Studies.

Thomas, H. S. (2013). A dynamic profile: Perceptions and facts. In H. S. Thomas & C. Williams (Eds.), *Parents personalities and power: Welsh-medium schools in South-East Wales* (pp. 37–63). Cardiff: University of Wales Press.

Welsh Government (2015). *School census results 2015*. Cardiff: Welsh Government. Retrieved from http://gov.wales/docs/statistics/2015/150723-school-census-results-2015-en.pdf

Welsh Language Board. (1995). *Public attitudes to the Welsh language*. London: NOP.

Welsh Language Board. (1999). *The Welsh language: A vision and mission for 2000–2005*. Cardiff: Welsh Language Board.

Williams, G., Roberts, E., & Isaac, R. (1978). Language and aspirations for upward social mobility. In G. Williams (Ed.), *Social and cultural change in contemporary Wales* (pp. 193–205). London: Routledge and Kegan Paul.

Appendix. Construction of five dimensions

Dimension 1: demographic characteristics

A total of 11 additional variables were considered for inclusion in demographic characteristics. Six of these: sex, occupational sector (private, public, self-employed), household type (single-person household, one adult with children, two adults, two adults with children etc.), whether the respondent was married, whether the respondent had children, and whether the respondent had a disability, were not statistically significantly associated with the likelihood of choice of Gaelic-medium education (at the 10% significance level). Five variables were statistically significantly associated with the dependent variable, but measured similar demographics to those included in the model above. These were: household income, employment status (working, student, retired, unemployed), tenure of household, geographical area type (large urban to remote rural), and social class (using the National Statistics Socio-Economic Classification).

Dimension 2: exposure to Gaelic

Two additional variables were considered for inclusion in the 'exposure to Gaelic' group. The first, which reported on how often, if at all, respondents had visited the most strongly Gaelic-speaking areas of Scotland (covered by the council areas Comhairle nan Eilean Siar, Highland, and Argyll & Bute) within the previous 12 months was not statistically significantly associated with likelihood to choose Gaelic-medium education for a child. The second – respondents' speaking competencies in Gaelic – did return a statistically significant relationship with the dependent variable, but the 'speaking' variable was found to be highly correlated with the 'understanding' variable ($r = 0.784$, $p = .000$). 'Understanding' was chosen as the indicator variable for respondent Gaelic-language competence, as it was more strongly associated with the dependent variable.

Dimension 3: national and cultural identity

Four further variables were considered for inclusion within the national and cultural identity group. Two pertained to the place of Gaelic in Scottish cultural identity: namely the extent to which respondents' believe that speaking Gaelic is important to being Scottish, and the amount of similarity respondents' believe Gaelic speakers to have with other people in Scotland. Two pertained to politics: namely, respondents' party-political affiliations, and respondents' preferences regarding Scotland's constitutional future (Scotland in UK without own parliament, Scotland in UK with own parliament, Scotland not in UK). Although all of these variables were individually significantly related to the dependent variable, they did not hold additional statistically significant explanatory power when they were entered into the model along with the four explanatory variables included within Dimension 3 (detailed in Section 3.1).

Developing resources for translanguaging in minority language contexts: A case study of rapping in an Irish primary school

Máiréad Moriarty

ABSTRACT

The aim of the present study is to examine the extent to which pedagogic resources based on the principles of translanguaging provide an alternative approach to the teaching of language. The Irish language situation provides a good context in which to investigate the potential for transglossic resources to function as effective teaching resources because it is a situation where having access to the minority language via the education system has not resulted in frequent informal language use. The presence of the Irish language in the curriculum has undoubtedly helped develop competence; however, there is strong evidence to show that this competence is rarely activated outside of the classroom setting (cf. Moriarty, 2015). This article provides an analysis of a study on rap as a resource for a more flexible approach to the teaching of Irish. The data show that the use of transglossic resources does foster a more positive ideological position for the language both in the classroom and in the students' social environment. Also, it demonstrates the capacity of rap to provide a space in which even the most limited Irish language resources can be mobilised.

Introduction

Translanguaging is an emerging term within the study of bilingualism and particularly in the field of language education (cf. Blackledge & Creese, 2010; Creese & Blackledge, 2011; García, 2009; Wei, 2011; Williams, 1994). The number of studies which focus on the development of specific pedagogic resources to promote a more flexible approach to bilingualism in the classroom is minimal and it is at this gap in the available literature that the present study is aimed. This article focuses on the development of rap as a transglossic resource to be used in the teaching of Irish in primary schools. It is clear that the strict language separation favoured and promoted by the current educational policy that surrounds the teaching of Irish in State schools is at odds with the lived sociolinguistic reality of the Irish context. Arguably, the future viability of the Irish language demands a more flexible approach to its users and uses (cf. e.g. O'Rourke & Walsh, 2015 for a detailed account of new speakers of Irish). For this reason, the present study sets out to examine the extent to which creative pedagogic resources can function as a tool to promote a more

SUPPORT, TRANSMISSION, EDUCATION AND TARGET VARIETIES

flexible approach to the teaching of Irish through the adoption of a translanguaging norm over the parallel monolingualism (Kelly-Holmes, 2006) approach that has dominated Irish language education. The main objective of this study is to design and test locally viable translanguaging pedagogy from the ground up.

The article begins by tracing the origin of the term translanguaging and situating its development within the so-called dynamic turn in the study of bilingualism (cf. García & Wei, 2013). An account of the application of the term to the field of language education is then offered, together with a rationalisation for the use of rap as a transglossic resource for the promotion of a more fluid notion of languaging in the classroom. The study is then contextualised to the Irish situation and data from an initial phase of a larger project which investigates alternative ways to approach the teaching of Irish in schools is provided. The data presented here stem from one particular classroom and draw on the ideologies and language practices of the teacher and her pupils. Some possible implications of the findings, particularly in relation to effective language policy strategies in minority language education contexts, are discussed.

Translanguaging and minority languages

The strict separation of language codes is evident in the negativity that traditionally surrounded notions of code-switching and code-mixing, where all forms of language mixing were understood to be illustrative of a deficiency in one language code or another. In language policy discourses, language is put forward as a reified entity, yet when one examines the lived reality of language it rarely is produced in localised spaces of use in a pure or unified way. Lemke (2002) argues that by keeping languages pure and separate we do not promote multilingualism, but rather the simultaneous acquisition of two more language codes that remain separate This gave rise to a number of language pedagogies which promoted what Cummins (2005) describes as 'two solitudes'. The current trend which promotes the movement in the understanding of language as a fixed and static entity to a more malleable resource is captured in the term languaging (cf. Wei, 2011).

Since the turn of the twenty-first century, there has been an increase in the literature which takes a more flexible approach to bilingualism and multilingualism. This literature takes its starting point in the changing perceptions of what is said to constitute a language. The creation of fixed language categories such as English, French, Irish and so on is largely associated with development of Nationhood. As Bonfiglio (2010) contends, the codification of standardised languages allowed for the idea of citizenship based on proficiency in one language variety to dominate. A monolingual ideology developed in which language-based social structuring dominated. As Møller and Jørgensen (2009) argue: 'Along with norms of how "a language" can be used we find norms about who can use it, and to whom it belongs' (p. 145). As such the 'real' citizen spoke the normalised variety and ideology of deficiency was created round those who did not use the preferred variety. From here grew the idea of the monolingual norm and a subsequent framing of bilingualism from a monolingual perspective.

Two approaches to bilingualism developed from this perspective, namely subtractive and additive bilingualism. Subtractive bilingualism refers to a form of language health check where an individual's deficiency in the standard the language needed to be treated to the detriment of the language they used which was identified as inferior. Additive bilingualism, gave rise to what Heller (2006) referred to as double monolingualism, or parallel monolingualism as described by Kelly-Holmes (2006), in which individuals developed parallel skills in two or more languages. The societal consequences of such an approach to bilingualism are conceptualised through the notion of diglossia (Ferguson, 1959; Fishman, 1967). Diglossia is understood as a process through which some languages are seen as valuable in high or prestigious domains of language use and others are usable in low domains of language use. A common theme runs through these approaches to bilingualism, which is the notion of bilingualism as a functional separation of two distinct language codes. Recent theorising in the field of applied and socio-linguistics has highlighted the reductive nature of such a position and scholars are advocating for a shift to a more dynamic and flexible approach to bilingualism, where language is identified as a malleable resource. Blommaert (2010) calls for a shift in the perception of language as one single unitary code to a set of heteroglossic practices where language refers to a fluid and dynamic process in which individuals make use of various linguistic resources in their repertoire. A more fluid account of language moves language out of the restrictive characterisation and takes on an agentive quality, which in turn has given rise to the term languaging. Gort and Sembiante (2015) describe languaging as: '(...) a concept that emphasizes the agency of language users as they utilize semiotic resources as their disposal in strategic ways to communicate and act in the world' (p. 1).

With the rising awareness of the potential limitations associated with conceptualising language on an ideological level which is monoglossic in nature came a number of theoretical concepts to account for the dynamism associated with heterogolossic approaches to language. Some of these terms include: translanguaging (Blackledge & Creese, 2010; García, 2009; Williams, 1994) polylanguaging (Jørgensen, 2008), metrolingualism (Otsuji & Pennycook, 2010) and translingualism (Canagarajah, 2013). While each of these terms has made a significant contribution to the advancement of this approach of viewing language as a dynamic process of languaging, I wish to single out two terms in particular. The first is translanguaging, and given its prominence in the present study, a more detailed account is outlined below. However, the term polylanguaging and the adoption of the turn to polylingualism are also useful in understanding what fluid languaging encapsulates. Møller and Jørgensen (2009, 146) describe the polylingual norm as follows:

> language users employ whatever linguistic features are at their disposal to achieve their communicative aims as best they can, regardless of how much they know from the involved sets of features (e.g. 'languages'); this entails that the language users may know – and use – the fact that some of the features are perceived by some speakers as not belonging together and some features are assumed to belong to sets of features to which the speaker has no access.

While these terms offer a new perspective on language, they have received some criticism over the focus on urban settings. For example, Canagarajah (2013) argues: '(...) the suggestion that translanguaging practices are postmodern and urban can give a misleading impression, and hide their vibrancy in other places' (p. 3). The term metrolingualism in particular seems to provide little space for the examination of languaging practices in rural areas, where often minority and endangered languages exist. The transformation in the conceptualisation of a language has consequences for all languages and given the focus here is specifically on endangered minority languages the term translanguaging is favoured here, as it is a more all-encompassing term.

Translanguaging

As is widely documented in the ever-increasing literature on translanguaging (cf. Lewis, Jones, & Baker, 2012 for an account of the rise of translanguaging research), its origins are in the Welsh context where Williams (1994) used the term to describe the type of language use that pupils attending bilingual schools in Wales were exhibiting. This sense of the term promotes a particular pedagogical practice where both the Welsh and English languages are used interchangeably in order to promote dual language acquisition. Williams (2003) suggested that translanguaging often uses the stronger language to develop the weak language, thus contributing to a potentially relatively balanced development of a child's two languages. As Gorter (2015) suggests, the pedagogic approach to translanguaging was simply adopting the language practices the students exhibit in their own everyday languaging to the language class. Scholars such as García (2009) and García and Wei (2013) have broadened the scope of the term beyond the classroom but also beyond the association of the term with two languages. The significance of this broadening of the term to societal languaging is evident in Wei's (2011, p. 1223) account of translanguaging as a transformative act, one that:

> (…) creates a social space for the multilingual language user by bringing together different dimensions of their personal history, experience and environment, their attitude, beliefs and ideology, their cognitive and physical capacity into one coordinated and meaningful performance, and make it into a lived experience.

One field in which there has been a theoretical as well as an empirical shift in terms of the application of a translanguaging approach is that of language and education. Scholars such as Blackledge and Creese (2010); Cenoz and Gorter (2015); Flores and García, (2013); García (2009) and García and Wei (2013) have looked at how students and/or pupils make use of translanguaging practices both inside and outside of the classroom. The adoption of translanguaging pedagogy has the potential to offer a 'safe space' (Auer, 2010) in which a teacher can: 'meaningfully educate when they draw upon the full linguistic repertoire of all students, including language practices that are multiple and hybrid' (García & Kleifgen, 2010, p. 43).

Translanguaging and Irish language pedagogy

SLA and language pedagogy research has traditionally promoted the use of the target language only in second language research. Many of the researchers promoting translanguaging as an alternative means through which everyday language practices can be examined and taught highlight the distinctive need to move beyond the strict compartmentalisation of languages. There is an ever-increasing volume of literature which argues for the move away from the separation of languages in the classroom to the use of two or more languages in the same lesson (cf. Baker, 2010; Blackledge & Creese, 2010; Cenoz & Gorter, 2015; García, 2009). The translanguaging frame provides an opportunity to move away from looking at language practices, such as code-switching, as potentially damaging to language competence, to a more fluid approach which identifies bilingualism as a flexible resource. Otheguy, García, and Reid (2015) refer to translanguaging as the use of an individual's idiolect, that is, their linguistic repertoire without adhering to socially and often politically defined labels or language boundaries. The practical application of translanguaging means that one can adopt language resources without full or perfect competence. This is significant in the case of minority language studies as it reconstitutes what it means to be a speaker and gives legitimacy to the language practices of non-traditional users whose knowledge of the respective language may be limited.

Translanguaging and minority languages

Translanguaging offers an opportunity for minority language revitalisation efforts to rethink the ideology surrounding who gets to be a user of a given minority language. Otheguy et al. (2015) argue that a translanguaging approach to minority language revitalisation 'allows us to graduate from the goal of "language maintenance", with its constant risk of turning minoritisied languages into museum pieces, to that of sustainable practices by bilingual speakers (…)' (p. 283).

The various categorisations available for minority languages place them on a continuum from full health to endangered to approaching imminent death. Yet, this minority language health rater is often based on a monolingual fallacy where much of the statistics used to classify minority languages on specific points on this continuum is drawn from data taken from so-called L1 users of such languages. While I do not wish to undermine the validity of looking at minority languages in this way, it is clear that such an approach does not take into account changes in what constitutes language use evident in the fluid and dynamic language practices apparent in today's society. Perhaps a more useful way to approach minority language revitalisation is to examine the spaces and places in which varying uses of Irish language resources are present (to include instances of borrowing and code-mixing and code-switching). A degree of 'truncated competence' (Blommaert, Collins, & Slembrouck, 2005) carries value in situations of minority language preservation. In what follows, I promote rap as a potential resource for the promotion of a more flexible approach to the teaching of minority languages like Irish, in which hybrid language use (translanguaging) is promoted as 'normal'.

Rap as a translanguaging resource in minority language education

Recent studies on minority languages such as Sámi, Irish, Maya (cf. Cru, 2015; Moriarty, 2011) have demonstrated a growth in the use of these languages in domains of popular culture and the potential for changes on the level of language ideologies and practices. Spaces of popular culture, such as social media sites, represent domains in which translanguaging are evident (Moriarty, 2015). Many scholars have shown how flexible and highly creative semiotic practices are evident in these domains. The playful and creative language use that is evident in Twitter, for example, is indicative of translanguaging as it is a space where language resources are mobile and fluid. The benefits of the use of minority languages in the space can be traced to the role of youth in such genres. As Tulloch (2014) argues rap is a space where youth's voice, choice and agency are brought in to play.

As I have argued elsewhere (Moriarty, 2015), rap is a linguistic and cultural phenomenon which holds a key to enabling minority languages to enter a globalised culture of modernity. Pennycook (2007, p. 112) contends: 'much of Hip Hop challenges ortholinguistic practices and ideologies relocating language in new ways, both reflecting and producing local language practices'. Rap provides a space in which the fluid and porous use of multiple linguistic resources are present, thus signifying a space in which the penalisation of hybrid language use is avoided and gets promoted as the norm. Rap promotes a translanguaging approach while simultaneously breaking up the fixed traditional attitudes and ideologies; hence the identification of rap as a space where linguistic and cultural resources are blended and appropriated in translocal environments. It offers the chance to build teachable pedagogic resources which encourage students to add new language practices to their linguistic repertoires, a point examined with respect to the Irish context in the remainder of this article.

The Irish language context

As many accounts of the sociolinguistic context of Ireland (cf. Moriarty, 2015) have shown, a discourse of language death prevails and many people question the resources that are spent each year on maintaining the language. In spite of this Irish remains an important marker of identity and the general ideological standing is quite strong. Like many other minority language contexts, there is a discourse of purism that surrounds those who constitute 'Irish speakers'. As I have argued elsewhere, those to whom the label of legitimate Irish speaker is conferred can be divided into three categories: the traditional Gaeltacht user; the militant gaelgoirí or upper middle class Gaelscoil users. In more recent times scholars such as O'Rourke and Walsh (2015) have begun to investigate what they term 'new speakers' of Irish. They define the new speaker as 'those individuals who acquired the language outside of the home and who report that they use Irish with fluency, regularity and commitment' (p. 64). Their research points to a growth in the urban proliferation of new speakers and they refer to a particular type of Irish language user, one who has made a conscious decision to make more frequent use of their Irish language resource, a process which is akin to the notion of a 'mude' as discussed vis-à-vis the Catalan context in Pujolar and Puigdevall (2015). The inclusion of such non-traditional users is a welcome addition to the label of Irish speaker, yet an even more flexible approach could perhaps widen the net even further. After all, 'Language is something done in a particular time and space (Pennycook, 2010, p. 12) and as such new speakers can be seen to be "doing" language across new time-space dimensions by actively creating or constructing new linguistic identities' (O'Rourke & Walsh, 2015, p. 70).

Irish language policy: A focus on the education system

At the core of what can be said to constitute a language policy in Ireland is a focus on language acquisition via the educational system (Coady & Ó Laoire, 2002). Early Irish language planners envisaged the educational system as holding the key to the revival of the Irish language as schools were one of the major agents that facilitated the shift to English. Many of these early approaches were focused on reordering the diglossic status quo where Irish would replace English as the H language, or even more unrealistic was the expectation that there would be a full reversion to a monolingual Irish-speaking Ireland. Of course much of the rationale for this stemmed from the fact that many other European states had been formed in this way and to be a true Irish nation the island needed to be Irish speaking. Several decades of language acquisition via the educational system have not resulted in an active use of the language in everyday society. Kelly (2002), who examined the achievements of the compulsory Irish policy (until 1973), found the lack of a speech community was hindering the success of Irish language revival via the educational system. He argues that 'The problem was that schoolchildren and their parents realised there were limited opportunities to use Irish in the broader society, while teachers themselves were the only group charged with effecting the revival' (Kelly, 2002, p. 103). Having access to the minority language has not resulted in informal language use. Even in Irish medium schools there is a strong tendency for pupils to switch to English once they leave the classroom (cf. Coady & Ó Laoire, 2002). This is not to undermine the fact that the education system has been successful in developing minority language competence. There has been a steady growth in secondary bilinguals and without government intervention at the level of acquisition language planning it is unlikely the language would have survived to the same capacity as it has done today (cf. Ó hIfearnáin, 2000).

Notably, one of the contradictions highlighted by an examination of data on the Irish language question in the census is that the number of people who claim to have some ability in the language has increased, but that the number of people who use it is declining. This highlights how misleading census data can be. Ó Murchú (2001, p. 67) suggests that:

> Referring to those professing ability to speak Irish as Irish speakers is misleading since a large proportion of them never use, or have access to contexts in which they might use that ability. They are potential rather than actual speakers. (quoted in Walsh 2011, p. 28)

It would seem that the positioning of Irish language competence in this way is firmly rooted in outdated approaches as to what constitutes a speaker of Irish. A more fluid interpretation would allow for whom hitherto have not been identified as Irish speakers to make use of the Irish language resources they have, however minimal, in a way that was meaningful to them. The reality is that users of Irish frequently translanguage. It is fair to say that the Irish language speech community is one in which the Irish and English languages are not seen as discrete and separate languages, as is exemplified in the high proportion of 'Irishising' of English words, for example, the use of *mo bhicycle* for bicycle instead of the formal word *rothár*. O'Malley-Madec (2007) found highly frequent use of English discourse markers such as yeah, now etc. in Gaeltacht speech.

In the Irish sociolinguistic context there is a distinct need to move beyond the compartmentalisation of languages. The education system has offered a formal domain for the acquisition of Irish. As an official domain for language policy, the education system focuses on enacting language policy measures which are unidirectional, that is, come from the top-down. As many accounts of language policy and planning in educational settings across the globe have found, schools also have the potential to function as bottom-up language policy agents. Johnson (2010) examines and explores spaces for educator agency. Hornberger (2010, pp. 562–563) highlights the need to develop: 'sociolinguistically informed educators …[who can] open up ideological and implementational space for multilingualism and social justice, from the bottom-up'. Flores and Schissel (2014) draw on Hornberger's (2005) distinction between ideological spaces and implementational spaces as means through which those involved in language education can conceptualise and create classroom environments that make use of translanguaging. They highlight the need for those involved in language education initiatives to '(…) create ideological spaces that move away from monoglossic language ideologies toward heterogolossic language ideologies and

SUPPORT, TRANSMISSION, EDUCATION AND TARGET VARIETIES

implementational spaces that provide concrete tools for enacting this vision in the classroom' (Flores & Schissel, 2014, p. 454). Before such an approach can gain real currency, there needs to be 'safe spaces' (Auer, 2010) where such languaging is favoured and used. Perhaps it may be more productive for teachers involved in the teaching of the Irish language to use a blend of monolingual usage and concurrent usage (translanguaging) to help pupils make use of existing language knowledge in the acquisition of Irish. Rap provides one potential resource that could be used to build translanguaging pedagogy.

In the next section, data from a larger-scale project examine the extent to which teachers use translanguaging resources in the classroom and how successful they are amongst pupils. The larger project to which the data belong is a case study which examines the design and implementation of pedagogic resources for translanguaging in the Irish context. The study is comparative in nature in that it contrasts the effectiveness of these tools in two separate primary schools in Ireland, one of which is an English medium school where Irish is a curricular subject and a second school which is an Irish language immersion school.

Assessing rap as a pedagogic resource for translanguaging

The data discussed in this article was collected using an integrative ethnographic approach (Castanheira, Crawford, Dixon, & Green, 2001). I made use of ethnographic methods which included classroom observations, a semi-structured teacher interview, informal discussions and video recordings of lessons using the translanguaging approach. The data on which the discussion is based stem from (a) two interviews with a primary school teacher, (b) five classroom observations of Irish lessons, (c) video recordings of the children rapping and (d) informal conversations with the teacher and pupil, before, during and after the implementation of rap as a pedagogic resource to promote translanguaging.

The school for which the data presented here is concerned with is an English medium school located in the South West of the country. The school is categorised as a DEIS school (Delivering Equality of Opportunity in Schools). The DEIS programme, which was introduced by the Department of Education and Science (DES) in 2006/2007, is aimed at addressing the educational needs of children and young people from disadvantaged communities. A large percentage of the student body are from disadvantaged backgrounds and the school is categorised by large-scale diversity in terms of the nationalities attending the school. With such diversity comes the possibility for a rich multilingual environment and for this reason the school offers an ideal locus for the examination of transglossic rap as a means to promote a more favourable attitude to the use of Irish linguistic resources, as well as resources from other languages. Table 1 presents a breakdown of the languages spoken by the children in the particular class the data pertains to. Unsurprisingly, the majority of children reported using English only. A total of four students reported some use of Irish outside of school. One child was from an Irish-speaking background where Irish was the L1 of the home and the other three children reported a strong knowledge of Irish as they attend an Irish medium pre-school, Naíonra. The label of multilingual refers to the use of 12 languages amongst 8 of the pupils. This breaks down as three Polish-speaking children, two Arabic-speaking children who reported using more than one variety of Arabic and two children from Nigeria who reported speaking French, English and a variety of indigenous Nigerian languages.

SUPPORT, TRANSMISSION, EDUCATION AND TARGET VARIETIES

Table 1. Language diversity amongst the pupils ($N = 34$).

English-only	22
English mainly, some Irish	4
Multilingual	8

Teacher experience of teaching Irish

Following an initial agreement to take part in the study, I interviewed the teacher in question to ascertain her attitude to the Irish language, to teaching the language and to get her opinion on the pupils' attitude to the language. The teacher reported herself as having a good level of Irish. Before moving to this school she had spent some time teaching in an Irish medium school and is from a background which she says has always had an interest in Irish language and culture. She describes herself as enthusiastic about the language and describes Irish as one of her more favourite subjects to teach. When asked in an interview about her view of her pupils' attitude to the language she made the comment mentioned in Figure 1.

Throughout the interview the teacher positions herself as curator of a museum piece. She reports that she and her colleagues are faced with negativity from both pupils and parents when it comes to the teaching of Irish. She spoke about the constant backlash she receives from parents when the topic of how well their children are doing is broached in parent/teacher meetings with parents viewing the teaching of the language as a waste of the limited resources available to the school. The challenge facing them as teachers is ideological but also practise based. The teacher also reported that even pupils who have a strong favourable attitude to the language and are competent users have no space to use the language and their current enthusiasm for the language will be short-lived.

The teacher was enthusiastic when the possibility of developing and using more flexible language learning resources was put to her. She was for the use of rap as a trans-languaging resource and saw the potential benefit in approaching the teaching of language differently. She said: 'the class will be concentrating on creating a rap and they may not see it as the same old boring Irish lesson'. The teacher came up with the idea of allowing the children to perform the rap for the school and their parents at the end of the school play. She felt this would give the students the added incentive to take it seriously, but also provide them with the motivation to impress others.

After the initial enthusiasm came a worry of how the teacher would actually go about doing this in her classroom. It was imperative that if we were going to develop a set of

---

I really see the value of Irish and I would really love it if my students would grow fond of it, you know. I would say that mostly my Irish lesson is met the grunts and groans and questions of 'why do we have to do Irish teacher' its so boring and nobody speaks it anyway. I think the kids attitude is reflective of what they hear at home or ideas they get more generally about the language. For the most part pupils see it as insignificant, useless, as having little value outside the classroom and certainly no real for them outside the class

Figure 1. Teacher's account of pupils' attitude to learning Irish.

SUPPORT, TRANSMISSION, EDUCATION AND TARGET VARIETIES

Table 2. Rules for rapping.

1. Students could discuss the content of what was going into the rap using English
2. The rap had to be written in Irish mainly, but students could use resources from other languages
3. Students had to write a short narrative piece on their experience over the eight-week period

resources which used translanguaging pedagogically we need to ensure the lessons allowed for every student to use their entire linguistic repertoire irrespective of whether the teacher or indeed the student would position themselves on a bilingual continuum. In order to achieve this goal, we came to a mutual consensus that specific activities would be targeted to improve specific skills in Irish so that the teacher could allay her fear of not meeting the targets directed to her from the curriculum. But it was also important that children from non-national backgrounds would be allowed to insert resources from languages they had knowledge of. Table 2 presents the rules for rapping.

The reasons for the three 'rules' presented in Table 2 to be the core for the teacher are as follows. Firstly, by allowing students to discuss the task using English she would avoid any possible reluctance to be involved and she felt it would be more inclusive. Secondly, insisting that the rap be written largely in Irish, the development of key literacy skills would be ensured and the development of oral proficiency would come through the performance. Lastly, the specific narrative task was the teacher's own to test to see if there would be evidence of any spontaneous use of the language following the eight-week period. The pupils had autonomy over the content of the rap and they chose it as a space to argue for better school tours. In that way the pupils were also staying true to the ethos of rap, as a space for youth voice and agency.

An initial analysis of the video recordings of the pupils working on their rap would show that they translanguaged frequently. It was a very active learning environment with lots of creative play with language resources from the languages spoken by all the children in the class. The rap they produced was predominately in Irish, but it included frequent *code-meshing* (cf. Canagarajah, 2011) with English and scarce use of Polish, French and a Nigerian indigenous language was present. An important factor for the teacher, who was taking the risk of using this flexible approach to meet the criteria vis-à-vis the Irish language curriculum, was the students were languaging appropriately for their level. That being said, the students did not have the requisite competence for there to be seamless fluidity between languages but students were certainly demonstrating a more flexible approach to using language resources that I had noted in previous observations of the class.

Reactions to the use of rap as a resource for translanguaging

Both the teacher and her pupils responded positively to the overall experience. Tables 3 and 4 present some of the comments the teacher and her pupils made during an informal review session we had.

Table 3. Teacher's experience of rap as a translanguaging resource.

Pupils have more confidence to use even the smallest amount of their language
It has helped even the quietest pupil find their tongue
What has amazed me is how this approach has helped the non-national children in my class. They are so excited to have their mother tongue used in the class and they are certainly more engaged with both English and Irish.
I think everyone wins with this approach. I win as there is a buzz around the subject, the strong students win as they are acting as teachers to their peers and the weak students have a space where their very limited capacity can be put to use

SUPPORT, TRANSMISSION, EDUCATION AND TARGET VARIETIES

Table 4. Pupils' experience of rap as a translanguaging resource.

It was so much fun. So much better the our other Irish lessons
Before I never put my hand up when teacher asked a question in Irish. I didn't like speaking Irish and I was afraid I would get it wrong
Irish is my favourite thing at school and I love it even more now.
I didn't know learning Irish could be so much fun

It would seem that from both the perspective of the teacher and the pupils the overall experience was very positive. Students with all levels of ability in Irish made use of their Irish language resources. An ideological shift, where Irish moved from a subject identified as boring with old fashioned learning methods and materials, was evident. The pupils themselves reported a change in how they viewed the language. It gained some currency through the fun and innovative teaching method which allowed them to create a rap about a topic that was important to them and they gained kudos from the other school children at the end of the term.

Overall, the series of lessons taken up by the rap task provided students with a safe space in which to play with their language skills where the pupils were enabled to practising bilingualism. Both the teacher and the pupils attested to a transformation in their Irish lesson from *"unpleasant atmosphere"* to quote the teacher, to one which was lively, engaging and focused more on being creative with their collective language skills than focusing on the acquisition of Irish. The rap task offered the pupils a chance to move away from their Irish language textbook that had limited applicability to the everyday lives of children from severely disadvantaged backgrounds to a space where they visibly enjoyed. Students were empowered and as a result acquired more language knowledge than in the Irish lessons they had experienced hitherto. Their languaging skills were not the only skills such an approach was benefitting. It also thought the children how to achieve something as a group and forced them to think creatively. This phase of the wider project illustrates the potential for the classroom to become a space where a more positive ideological orientation to the Irish language is created as well as to languages more generally.

Discussion

The present study addresses Lin and Martin's (2005) call for research to explore teachable resources for the development of a more flexible approach to language teaching. This short study of an Irish classroom as shown that rap offers a resource for the development of a transglossic pedagogy in minority language education. Based on the principles of translanguaging rap offers a 'safe space' in which a more holistic approach to language education seems to have a more positive outcome. As the results indicate, the positive impact seems largely to be on the level of ideology.

There is strong evidence from this case study to suggest that experience of developing a rap was an empowering experience for the school children involved. It legitimised students' language practices despite how their competence is recognised according to specific testing mechanisms. Similarly, the classroom studied here is a space where multiple language resources became an asset to achieving a group aim and students' confidence was strengthened and all of the language resources were provided a space in which they were valued. I would contend that the identification of rap as a transglossic space also offers the potential to overcome the ghettoisation of migrant school children in Irish primary schools.

In the Irish sociolinguistic context there is a distinct need to move beyond the compartmentalisation of languages. The education system has offered a formal domain for the acquisition of Irish. As an official domain for language policy, the education system focuses on enacting language policy measures which are unidirectional, that is, come from the top-down. The results of the initial phase of this project have demonstrated teachers need to provide an ideological orientation that favours a flexible approach to languaging rather that one which is predisposed to parallel monolingualism. After all, if languages like Irish are to survive in the future there is a need for voices to be valued.

Conclusion

There is a need to overcome the monolingual mind-set that has underpinned much of the existing approaches to minority language education. The present study did not intend to dismiss previous work that has been done on minority language policy within the educational domain. Many such policies were developed at a time when conceptualisation of bilingualism operated within the dual monolingualism mentality. Language education policies in European minority language contexts have secured such languages by developing language competence within the formal education system. Yet, such approaches rarely promote a fluid or flexible approach to language and are often at odds with the everyday reality of minority language use.

There is a need for the educational system to become both an ideological and an implementational space where flexible bilingualism is supported via language practices that constitute translanguaging. Language in education policies needs to be adopted in order to accommodate for these shifts in the conceptualisations of language and move away from an approach that does not favour standard language ideologies or idealise the so-called native speaker. By and large, monoglossic language ideologies seem to underpin current approaches for educational language policy in Ireland. There is a need for what happens at the level of community language use to be reflected in the classroom. Teachers need to be educated on how to develop the promotion of a flexible approach to Irish language teaching. By doing so, teachers can act on their agency as bottom-up language planners.

For Irish language revitalisation efforts to be truly successful in the long run there is a need for a radical reform of how the language is taught in schools. For this to happen there needs to be many changes on many different levels from teacher training, to the development of suitable pedagogic resources, to a change in assessment mechanisms to ensure that the assessment aligns with the heterogolossic approach. A more flexible approach which builds on students' real experiences of Irish can only stand to be of benefit to the continued maintenance of the language. The intention is not for the translanguaging resources to completely replace existing methods but to be used as an additional resource that can be used in conjunction with other methods in order to tackle the negativity that surrounds the teaching and learning of Irish. This would perhaps promote a more holistic approach to multilingual education as promoted by Cenoz and Gorter (2011).

Disclosure statement

No potential conflict of interest was reported by the author.

References

Auer, P. (2010). *Language and space: An international handbook of linguistic variation. Theories and methods* (Vol. 1). New York, NY: Walter de Gruyter.

Baker, C. (2010). Increasing bilingualism in bilingual education. In D. Morris (Ed.), *Welsh in the 21st century* (pp. 61–79). Cardiff: University of Wales Press.

Blackledge, A., & Creese, A. (2010). *Multilingualism: A critical perspective.* London: Continuum.

Blommaert, J. (2010). *The sociolinguistics of globalization.* Cambridge: Cambridge University Press.

Blommaert, J., Collins, S., & Slembrouck, S. (2005). Polycentricity and interactional regimes in global neighbourhoods. *Ethnography, 6,* 205–235.

Bonfiglio, T. (2010). *Mother tongues and nations.* New York, NY: Walter de Gruyter.

Canagarajah, S. (2011). Translanguaging in the classroom: Emerging issues for research and pedagogy. *Applied Linguistics Review, 2*(1), 1–28.

Canagarajah, S. (2013). *Translingual practice: Global Englishes and cosmopolitan relations.* New York: Routledge.

Castanheira, M. L., Crawford, T., Dixon, C. N., & Green, J. L. (2001). Interactional ethnography: An approach to studying the social construction of literate practices. *Linguistics and Education, 11*(4), 353–400.

Cenoz, J., & Gorter, D. (2011). A holistic approach to multilingual education: Introduction. *The Modern Language Journal, 95*(3), 339–343.

Cenoz, J., & Gorter, D. (2015). *Multilingual education.* Cambridge: Cambridge University Press.

Coady, M., & Ó Laoire, M. (2002). Mismatches in the policy and the practice: The case of Gaelscoileanna in the Republic of Ireland. *Language Policy, 1*(2), 143–158.

Creese, A., & Blackledge, A. (2011). Ideologies and interactions in multilingual education: What can an ecological approach tell us about bilingual pedagogy? In C. Hélot & M. Ó Laoire (Eds.), *Language policy for the multilingual classroom: Pedagogy of the possible* (pp. 3–21). Clevedon: Multilingual Matters.

Cru, J. (2015). Bilingual rapping in Yucatán, Mexico: Strategic choices for Maya language legitimation and revitalisation. *International Journal of Bilingual Education and Bilingualism,* 1–16. http://dx.doi.org/10.1080/13670050.2015.1051945

Cummins, J. (2005). *Teaching for cross-language transfer in dual language education: Possibilities and pitfalls. TESOL Symposium on Dual Language Education: Teaching and Learning Two Languages in the EFL Setting.* Retrieved from http://www.tesol.org/docs/defaultsource/new-resource-library/symposium-on-dual-language-education-3.pdf?sfvrsn=0

Ferguson, C. A. (1959). Diglossia. *Word, 14,* 47–56.

Fishman, J. A. (1967). Bilingualism with and without diglossia; diglossia with and without bilingualism. *Journal of Social Issues, 23*(2), 29–38.

Flores, N., & García, O. (2013). Linguistic third spaces in education: Teacher's translanguaging across the bilingual continuum. In D. Little, C. Leung, & P. Van Avermaet (Eds.), *Managing diversity in education: Key issues and some respones* (pp. 245–256). Clevedon: Multilingual Matters.

Flores, N., & Schissel, J. L. (2014). Dynamic bilingualism as the norm: Envisioning a heteroglossic approach to standards-based reform. *TESOL Quarterly, 48*(3), 454–479.

García, O. (2009). *Bilingual education in the 21st century: A global perspective.* Oxford: Wiley-Blackwell.

García, O., & Kleifgen, J. A. (2010). *Educating emergent bilinguals: Policies, programs, and practices for English language learners.* New York, NY: Teachers College Press.

García, O., & Wei, L. (2013). *Translanguaging: Language, bilingualism and education.* Basingstoke: Palgrave Macmillan.

Gort, M., & Sembiante, S. F. (2015). Navigating hybridized language learning spaces through translanguaging pedagogy: Dual language preschool teachers' languaging practices in support of emergent bilingual children's performance of academic discourse. *International Multilingual Research Journal, 9*(1), 7–25.

Gorter, D. (2015). Multilingual interaction and minority languages: Proficiency and language practices in education and society. *Language Teaching, 48*(1), 82–98.

Heller, M. (2006). *Linguistic minorities and modernity: A sociolinguistic ethnography*. London: Continuum.

Hornberger, N. (2005). Opening and filling up implementational and ideological spaces in heritage language education. *Modern Language Journal, 89*, 605–612.

Hornberger, N. (2010). Language and education: A limpopo lens. In N. H. Hornberger & S. McKay (Eds.), *Sociolinguistics and language education* (pp. 549–563). Clevedon: Multilingual Matters.

Johnson, D. C. (2010). Implementational and ideological spaces in bilingual education language policy. *International Journal of Bilingual Education and Bilingualism, 13*(1), 61–79.

Jørgensen, J. (2008). Polylingal languaging around and among children and adolescents. *International Journal of Multilingualism, 5*(3), 161–176.

Kelly, A. (2002). *Compulsory Irish: Language and education in Ireland 1870's–1970's*. Dublin: Irish Academic Press.

Kelly-Holmes, H. (2006). Multilingualism and commercial language practices on the Internet. *Journal of Sociolinguistics, 10*, 507–519.

Lemke, J. (2002). Becoming the village: Education across lives. In G. Wells & G. Claxton (Eds.), *Learning for life in the 21st Century* (pp. 34–45). Oxford: Blackwell.

Lewis, G., Jones, B., & Baker, C. (2012). Translanguaging: Developing its conceptualisation and contextualisation. *Educational Research and Evaluation, 18*(7), 655–670.

Lin, A., & Martin, P. (Eds.). (2005). *Decolonisation, globalisation: Language-in education policy and practice*. Clevedon: Multilingual Matters.

Møller, J. S., & Jørgensen, J. N. (2009). From language to languaging: Changing relations between humans and linguistic features. *Acta Linguistica Hafniensia, 41*(1), 143–166.

Moriarty, M. (2011). Minority languages and performative genres: The case of Irish language stand-up comedy. *Journal of Multilingual and Multicultural Development, 32*(6), 547–559.

Moriarty, M. (2015). *Globalising language policy and planning: An Irish language perspective*. Basingstoke: Palgrave Macmillan.

Otheguy, R., García, O., & Reid, W. (2015). Clarifying translanguaging and deconstructing named languages: A perspective from linguistics. *Applied Linguistics Review, 6*(3), 281–307.

Otsuji, E., & Pennycook, A. (2010). Metrolingualism: Fixity, fluidity and language in flux. *International Journal of Multilingualism, 7*(3), 240–254.

Ó hifearnáin, T. (2000). Majority and minority in language policy in Ireland. In E. Vēbers (Ed.), *Integrācija un Etnopolitika* (pp. 251–267). Rīga: Jumava/ Latvijas Universitātes Filozofijas un socioloģijas institūts.

O'Malley-Madec, M. (2007). How one word borrows another: The process of language-contact in two Irish-speaking communities. *International Journal of Bilingual Education and Bilingualism, 10*(4), 494–509.

Ó Murchú, M. (2001). *Chuman Buan Choimeádtana Gaelige: Tús an athréimnthe*. Baile Átha Cliath: Cois Teoranta.

O'Rourke, B., & Walsh, J. (2015). New speakers of Irish: Shifting boundaries across time and space. *International Journal of the Sociology of Language, 231*, 63–83.

Pennycook, A. (2007). *Global Englishes and transcultural flows*. London: Routledge.

Pennycook, A. (2010). *Language as a local practice*. London: Routledge.

Pujolar, J., & Puigdevall, M. (2015). Linguistic mudes: How to become a new speaker in Catalonia. *International Journal of the Sociology of Language, 2015*(231), 167–187.

Tulloch, S. R. (2014). Igniting a youth language movement. Inuit youth as agents of circumpolar language planning. In L. Wyman, T. McCarty, & S. Nicholas (Eds.), *Indigenous youth and multilingualism. Language identity, ideology, and practice in dynamic cultural worlds* (pp. 149–167). New York, NY: Routledge.

Walsh, J. (2011). *Contests and contexts: The Irish language and Ireland's socio-economic development*. Bern: Peter Lang.

SUPPORT, TRANSMISSION, EDUCATION AND TARGET VARIETIES

Wei, L. (2011). Moment analysis and translanguaging space: Discursive construction of identities by multilingual Chinese youth in Britain. *Journal of Pragmatics, 43*, 1222–1235.

Williams, C. (1994). *Arfarniado Ddulliau Dysguac Addysguyng Nghyddestun Addysg Uwchradd Ddwyieithog* (Unpublished PhD thesis). University of Wales Bangor.

Williams, C. (2003). Television and translanguaging in a bilingual teaching situation. In C. Bhushan Sharma (Ed.), *Technology enhanced primary education: Global experiences* (pp. 1–9). New Delhi: Kautilya.

Finding an ideological niche for new speakers in a minoritised language community

Michael Hornsby ⓘ

ABSTRACT
This article examines some of the linguistic and ideological tensions resulting from language shift and subsequent revitalisation, using Breton as a case study. As a result of the opening up of ideological spaces in discourses on what it means to be a Breton speaker in the twenty-first century, the appearance of so-called 'new' speakers highlights a number of points of contestation. Operating within contexts which are becoming increasingly 'postvernacular' [Shandler, J. (2004). Postvernacular Yiddish: Language as a performance art. *The DramaReview, 48*(1), 19–43; Shandler, J. (2006). *Adventures in Yiddishland: Postvernacular language and culture*. Oakland: University of California Press] in nature, the use of Breton by these speakers can be viewed as more symbolic rather than communicative in many respects. Postvernacular use exists on a continuum of linguistic practice and vernacular use of Breton is still apparent, of course, and often indexed as the only 'authentic' and legitimate use of Breton. This article examines some alternative linguistic practices within the Breton-speaking community and how 'new' speakers attempt to find for themselves an ideological niche in this community.

Introduction

Studies in obsolescent languages point to 'lead-in period to a language shift', which will affect the number of speakers and range of uses of a recessive language (Dorian, 1999, p. 99). Dorian has further suggested that language obsolescence is not a uniform process, pointing out that

> it seems time to acknowledge and set out the deviations from any imagined straight downward path of decline, lest the phenomena associated with language death and contraction be taken, quite erroneously, to be more obvious and less interesting than they actually are. (Dorian, 1986, p. 258)

This realisation has led researchers to identify linguistic practices which are more pragmatic and creative than previous studies might have suggested, in minority language communities such as Gaelic and French in Canada, as well as in Breton, the language in focus for the present article. In Cape Breton, Canada, for example, Mertz found that 'as Gaelic use ceases to serve as a regular medium for conveying semantico-referential information, it gains pragmatic force for expressing affect and creatively moulding the speech situation' (Mertz, 1989, p. 114). In other words, in a situation of rapid language shift, with 'an apparent yielding to hegemonic values, there may also be resistance and creativity' (Mertz, 1989, p. 115) which are manifest in boundary marking between insiders and outsiders to the community through the use of Gaelic, and through codeswitching to express emotion or humour (Mertz, 1989, pp. 113–114). These linguistic practices, restricted as they are in comparison to the use of Gaelic a generation or so previously, are part of a 'cultural-linguistic framework through which speakers actively interpret their linguistic experience which gives relative weight and meaning to particular linguistic usages' (Mertz, 1989, p. 113). In another setting in Canada, Heller (2003) found among minority French speakers in Ontario, 'tensions between the hybrid bilingualism which is the hallmark of [linguistic minorities] and the bounded monolingual-type performances they are usually asked to perform' (Heller, 2003, p. 490). These earlier studies pointed to the transformed use of varieties of Gaelic and French in a minoritised setting which suggested creative and adaptive ways speakers choose to deal with the realities of language shift.

In such situations, it is important to explore the role of language ideologies in processes of language shift and how these are mobilised by speakers with regard to the obsolescence or revitalisation of the recessive language. An ideology of language is generally considered to be 'the cultural system of ideas about social and linguistic relationships, together with their loading of moral and political interests' (Irvine, 1989, p. 255). The concept encompasses 'beliefs, or feelings, about languages as used in their social worlds' (Kroskrity, 2004, p. 498). By considering the various ideologies of language at play in a specific situation of language shift, we can uncover 'cultural conceptions of language – its nature, structure and use' (Woolard & Schieffelin, 1994, p. 55) and how these conceptions influence linguistic practices and attitudes. The analysis of language ideologies therefore offers us 'a set of powerful tools for modelling how and why linguistic choices, and the social valuation of these choices, vary across contexts' (Dickinson, 2010, p. 55). In particular, it is important to consider the distinctive roles of covert and overt ideologies of language in a situation of language shift. Covert ideologies of language influence 'subjective attitudes of a speech community towards its own and other languages are paramount for predicting language shift' (Grenoble & Whaley, 1998, p. 24), and are, as the term 'covert' suggests, acted upon unconsciously. Overt ideologies of language which feed into a general discourse are generally supportive of language revitalisation, and are actively drawn upon by speakers/users.

Analysing the underlying ideologies in situations of language obsolescence and revitalisation can help researchers and the speakers off minoritised languages better understand the dynamics and tensions within the language community. This article focuses on a number of ideological responses to the linguistic practices of contemporary Breton speakers and examines the ideological tensions which emerge between new and traditional speakers in relation to alternative, or postvernacular, ways of 'doing Breton'. In particular, the article examines how the process of postvernacularisation fits into a framework of language shift, taking Breton as a specific case study, and examining how ideological tension can arise in opposition to 'new' speakers and 'new' ways of speaking, connected with different aspects of language revitalisation. This tension can impede the acceptance

Postvernacularisation as a stage of language shift

One of the ways language communities experience shift and attrition is not only through the reduction and restriction in the domains of its use but also through its increased use as a marker of identity and a particular sociocultural stance rather than a medium of communication. Thus, the very act of speaking or using a minority language can take on new and adapted meanings, quite different from those that many older speakers grew up with. According to Shandler (2004), the communicative aspect of an exchange in an endangered language can be less important than the very act of speaking in and of itself:

> What engages my attention is the manner of their conversation: They are speaking rather too loudly for this sort of casual, intimate exchange; they are standing a bit too far apart from one another, their gestures are a bit too broad. They're not simply having a conversation in Yiddish; they're HAVING A CONVERSATION IN YIDDISH. They want others around them to notice. Indeed, it seems that they aren't (only) conversing, they are performing. (Shandler, 2004, p. 32)

This performative aspect, in the face of language decline but where group ethnicity is still vibrant (Glazer, 1980), runs the risk of tokenism, of course. However, as Edwards (2004) has pointed out, 'insufficient attention has been given to the continuing symbolic function of a language no longer spoken' (Edwards, 2004, p. 290). This kind of symbolic use can be viewed as postvernacular in nature, much as Shandler has suggested for the case of Yiddish, and which can be applied to many other cases of language minoritisation.

The term 'postvernacular' was first used by Shandler in an article in 2004 in reference to Yiddish and then in his book, *Adventures in Yiddishland*, published in 2008. A special edition of the *International Journal of the Sociology of Language* entitled *Breton: The Postvernacular Challenge* followed in 2013 (Hornsby & Vigers, 2013), exploring the ways in which Breton is being used in a postvernacular mode, even if this does not characterise all or even the majority of Breton linguistic practices at the present time. At its most basic, this poststructuralist term refers to the continuing use of a language in transformed and creative ways after most speakers have stopped speaking the language in question. Other authors such as Costa (2015) and Sallabank (2013) also make reference to postvernacularity when describing linguistic practices in lesser used languages such as Occitan and Guernesiais, respectively. It needs emphasising that many minority languages are certainly still community languages in their respective milieu – but they are also evolving and taking on traits of postvernacularity. In particular, such partial use is beginning to be the way many people come into contact with certain minority and heritage languages. The number of books which has appeared in recent decades detailing the comic (and hybrid) use of Yiddish, for example, is not inconsiderable; *The complete idiot's guide to learning Yiddish* by Blech (2000) encourages readers to learn 'some key phrases so you sound a little less goyish' (non-Jewish), styling itself to be 'a treasury of Yiddish words and phrases for everything' on its back cover. Note the reduction of language use to 'key phrases' and 'words and phrases'. This is very much in line with Shandler's view of postvernacular usage as 'not necessarily thought of, or even valued, as a separate, complete language' (Shandler, 2006, p. 194).

SUPPORT, TRANSMISSION, EDUCATION AND TARGET VARIETIES

The characterisation of a language in this way, not unsurprisingly, is often contested. Katz (2015) has seen the whole idea of postvernacularity as 'ridiculous as a word and as a concept' (Katz, 2015, p. 285), and sees 'the current intellectual environment [as] dominated by the post-vernacularists' (Katz, 2015, p. 286). He finds ridiculous the idea that the million or so Haredi (ultra-Orthodox) speakers of Yiddish should be labelled 'postvernacular':

> [T]here are multitudes of young Haredim who speak beautiful, rich Yiddish all day, though not the same exact dialect, grammar or spelling used by the academics when they 'play in Yiddish' or write each other Standard Yiddish emails in Latin letters, or culturists who write odes (in English) to the glories of Yiddish or the eternity of Yiddish. (Katz, 2015, p. 290)

In a similar way, Beer has expressed dissatisfaction with the concept: 'If Yiddish without Yiddish is a cultural phenomenon in its own right implying only a symbolic cultural identification or identity then both superficiality and ignorance are guaranteed outcomes' (Beer, 2009, p. 16). However, such practices are not a claim on vernacular domains since they represent more, I would argue, an expansion into a domain which is much more symbolic in nature, as Shandler has discussed:

> In semiotic terms, the language's primary level of signification - that is, its instrumental value as a vehicle for communicating information, opinions, feelings and ideas – is narrowing in scope. At the same time its secondary, or meta-level of signification – the symbolic value invested in the language apart from the semantic value of any given utterance in it is expanding. (Shandler, 2006, p. 4)

Postvernacularity can also be misunderstood as far as its relationship to vernacularity is concerned, since postvernacular use 'is a response or a reaction to [vernacular use] and exists on a dialogic, interdependent relationship with [the vernacular language]' (Shandler, 2006, p. 22). Thus, postvernacular use is not in competition with vernacular use – it is just a different, expanded use of the language, since it enriches rather than impoverishes, 'by opening up linguistic boundaries, thereby enabling a variety of engagements with the language, other than conventional fluency' (Shandler, 2006, p. 194). Understanding this would provide a richer explanation of the linguistic practices of some Yiddish speakers, which can be seen as 'idealization or reductionism' by some Yiddishists, for example, Beer (2009, p. 16). As Shandler (2006, p. 22) notes, postvernacular language does not supersede vernacular language, it acts more as a model for understanding language use in the era of late modernity; moreover, he argues 'not only that postvernacular Yiddish is dependent on vernacular Yiddish, past and present, but also that contemporary Yiddish culture is itself shaped in response to postvernacular phenomena' (Shandler, 2006, pp. 22–23).

Postvernacular use arises from overt ideologies of language. In a situation of language obsolescence, the conscious effort to use the recessive language in non-traditional ways, at different points on a scale or continuum of linguistic practice, involves positive attitudes towards the language and are located within an 'activist' framework. 'Activist' here is not understood particularly in militant terms (even though some speakers can engage in activities which are politically motivated, of course), but more in a pro-active engagement with the language they speak or are in the process of acquiring. This idea of postvernacularity being located in overt ideologies and positive language attitudes is explored in more depth in the next section, taking the basic premise of the concept described by Shandler

94

A minoritised language: the case of Breton

Breton, one of the regional languages of France, has undergone a dramatic decline in use throughout the course of the twentieth century and is an oft-repeated example in the literature of language attrition – see, for example, Mufwene (2004); Jones (1998); Tulloch (2006). Many studies point to the 1950s as a sort of 'tipping point', when intergenerational transmission basically broke down. Broudic (1995, p. 338) has shown that, in one township in Finistère over a period of less than ten years, Breton as the first language recorded for children entering the local school dropped from 100 to just 10%. A variety of factors seemed to have contributed to the continuing pattern of gradual language shift, such as migration and the drift from the land to jobs in the towns and the cities, since mechanisation had reduced the need for farm labour during the 1950s. Such transformations clearly weakened Breton, particularly in southwest Brittany, where industrialisation and urbanisation were more marked and where the tourist industry attracted a steady stream of monoglot French-speaking outsiders (Texier & Ó Néill, 2000, p. 5). Abalain (1989, p. 213) has suggested that out-migration from Brittany was encouraged by improvements in the road networks, and that the railways played an important role in language shift in Brittany, by allowing many Breton speakers to leave their normal places of residence in search of work in large urban centres in the rest of France. He claims those left behind started adopting an inferiority complex, as they compared their 'failure' in having stayed to the 'success' of those who had left, sometimes reinforced by the return of the latter in their retirement to the villages where they had been brought up. Paris was by far the preferred destination of many Breton émigrés, particularly young people and especially women, who found employment in cafés, restaurants and even as wet nurses. Traffic in the opposite direction brought in monolingual French speakers in the form of civil servants.

Methodology

Primary sources, in the form of (language) autobiographies and other narratives where minority language speakers discuss their experiences, enable us to put language shift into perspective and illustrate how people lived through social changes. They further document how negative ideologies and attitudes can be perpetuated and reproduced within a particular language community. This article draws on such sources to discuss the postvernacular use of Breton, and associated ideological tensions. A 'secondary analysis' approach has been adopted, which is a methodology for the study of non-naturalistic or artefactual data derived from previous studies and which has been recognised as having 'potential for re-using the various types of qualitative data produced in the course of social research, and to publish secondary studies using these resources' (Heaton, 2014, p. 6). In particular, Heaton further notes that 'life stories solicited for qualitative studies are unique data in that although they tend to be collected primarily for single use … are also recorded with the intention of archiving them for possible future use in other research' (Heaton, 2014, p. 6). Such 'life stories' relating to linguistic practices which are viewed as innovative (either by the speakers themselves or by others) are discussed in the following sections, and are drawn from a number of previously published resources (including autobiographical accounts and magazine articles), which were not specifically sociolinguistic in nature – yet, by adopting a secondary analysis approach, it has been possible to apply what Heaton (2014, p. 39) terms a 'supra analysis', or an analysis which involves 'the investigation of new theoretical, empirical or methodological questions' (Heaton, 2014).

A recent autobiographical volume by Cléac'h (2015), entitled 'The Dirty Little Breton' (*Le Sale Petit Breton*), in which he details his adolescence of the 1950s in La Forêt-Fouesnant and at school in Concarneau, describes a certain clash of civilisations between his rural origins and the town of his schooling. Cléac'h shows the disdain in which 'country hicks' were held in by those from the town, and the spread of so-called 'manners', or lifestyles, associated with urban living. This was accompanied by shifting tastes in clothing (p. 206) towards Parisian fashion and away from local Breton costume, the decline in popularity of traditional furniture (p. 208), the decline in agriculture as an economic practice (p. 210), and the waning influence of religion and the authority of 'an Aotrou Person', the parish priest, traditionally a key figure in social life in rural Brittany, much as in other rural societies (p. 209 and p. 217). As far as language is concerned, the superior attitude of monolingual French speakers towards bilinguals, the presence of linguistic enclaves (such as Concarneau) in an otherwise thoroughly Breton-speaking locality, all led to a sense of linguistic shame (p. 203) on the part of Breton speakers. What is particularly noticeable is that at the time, Breton speakers did not experience language shift as anything notable – it was part and parcel of a general trend towards modernisation: 'I don't think, like many others, I really thought about it at the time' (Cléac'h, 2015, p. 219, my translation). This is borne out by Ó hIfearnáin's (2014) observation that,

> communities that have undergone language shift from their traditional language to a dominant language often do not appreciate that their language is disappearing while the process is occurring, but instead only realize it when they notice that the younger generation can no longer communicate fluently in the ancestral language. (Ó hIfearnáin, 2014, p. 33)

Similarly to the Irish case which Ó hIfearnáin is basing his statement on, the shift away from Breton towards French in Brittany was driven through covert ideologies, the result of which – a break in intergenerational transmission – is still contested on many ideological, political and linguistic levels.

As a language in severe decline, the opportunities for speaking and using Breton are inexorably linked to the demographics of the current population of Breton speakers. Having fewer speakers means far fewer opportunities for using the language, of course, but on the other hand, it does mean that language users are not so restricted by community norms, as is often the case with more vigorous languages. In other words, language shift is producing new ideological spaces which are available for speakers to renegotiate how they perceive community norms to operate in relation to the minority language they speak, much as Armstrong (2012) has described in the case of three new Irish-language communities. This is not to say that contestation does not happen to a certain extent (see the section on Yiddish above), but the flip side of the coin is that the processes of language attrition can produce some unusual and creative outcomes. In particular, postvernacular use of minority languages can provide outlets for linguistic creativity at a particular stage of language attrition, as a parallel development to what Jones has described as 'the pre-terminal phase of some dying languages in particular socio-political contexts' (Jones, 1998, p. 323).

New speakers of Breton and ideological opposition

As previously mentioned, revitalising linguistic practices is the primary aim for some activists, whereas for others, keeping the idea of a language 'alive', even in symbolic form, is much more important. Thieberger (2002), for example, argues that a minority (language) identity can be successfully maintained through tokenistic practices, such as greetings. A continuum of linguistic practice thus emerges, which can be contested by different speakers holding different ideologies. For example, one new speaker, cited below, recalls the ideological barriers she encountered when speaking to her children in Breton in public:

> Les années où je parlais breton à mes enfants, je leur parlais aussi en public, évidemment, dans les magasins par exemple, mais j'ai essuyé plusieurs réflexions de gens qui me disaient que mon accent était drôle, que ça ne leur rappelait pas la langue de leur enfance (même des gens qui ne le parlaient plus). Ça me fait trop de peine, je suis déprimée après. C'est pour ça que j'ai arrêté.

> (During those years when I spoke Breton to my children, I used to speak to them in public as well, obviously, in the shops, for example, but I had to endure a number of comments of people who overheard who said my accent was funny, that the way I spoke didn't recall for them the language of their childhood (even from people who didn't speak it any longer). This was just too painful for me, and it depressed me afterwards. That's why I stopped.) (Hornsby, 2015, p. 57)

One of the Breton speakers interviewed in the 'Brud Nevez' journal makes an effort to speak Breton to her children, but says she will not force the issue:

> N'en em welan ket o komz en eur yezh all d'am bugale, ha pa vefen ma-unan o komz ar yez-se ganto … Med, n'in ket da dad-misioner war dachenn ar brezoneg. N'eo ket aze 'ma ma buhez.

> (I don't see myself speaking any other language to my children, and I normally use this language with them … But, I won't act as a missionary for Breton. That's not how my life is.) (Naoueg, 2009, p. 31)

Thus, while not exactly espousing direct ideologies which see the Breton language as 'dying' or of little use, these speakers are influenced by discourses of obsolescence to the extent that they question their own use and involvement with the language. They are, in that sense, reproducing or mirroring those prevalent ideologies which led to language shift in the first place. These ideologies can also be reproduced by outside commentators, who can question the linguistic output of certain categories of speaker and their place within the Breton-speaking community, as Hewitt, among others, has prophesised, since according to him, 'the Breton of the future in no way resembles the living language of traditional native speakers. It is no pleasant task to have to deliver this gloomy diagnosis and forecast' (Hewitt, in press).

Essentialist, purist ideologies of language seek to delegitimise the linguistic practices of new speakers of Breton as a group, without recognising that there are probably as many ways of speaking Breton as there are speakers and that a speaker can (and does) move on the previously mentioned continuum of linguistic practice. Le Pipec, acknowledging that new speakers of Breton can produce xenolects (slightly foreignised varieties) and endolects (more indigenous varieties), puts it thus:

> *Les néo-bretonnants, quant à eux, sont susceptibles de se déplacer à l'intérieur de ce continuum … Tel locuteur du xénolecte, estimant son parler inadéquat, peut s'appliquer à étudier la phonologie du breton et en acquérir les traits endogènes qui lui faisaient défaut. C'est le même chemin que suivent beaucoup d'apprenants, passant en quelques mois ou quelques années du néo-xénolecte à un néo-endolecte.*

> (New speakers of Breton are able to move between this continuum … A speaker of a xenolect variety, considering her own speech inadequate, can take up the study of Breton phonology and acquire the endogenous traits which are lacking. Many learners have followed this path, passing from a neo-xenolect to a neo-endolect in a few months or years.) (Le Pipec, 2013, pp. 113–114)

However, other Breton speakers can talk in terms which refer more positively to the idea that Breton is currently undergoing revitalisation. One speaker signals the necessity for the modernisation of Breton in the twenty-first century:

> *Sonjal a ra din ne zeuio ket ar brezoneg a-benn da dremen ar hantved-man ma ne ra ket gant binviou ar hehenti modern, ha ma ne vez ket greet dioutan eun nerz ekonomikel.*

> (I think that Breton won't survive this century if it doesn't come to terms with new ways of communication, and if it isn't made economically attractive.) (Gouvres, 2009, p. 29)

Another listed all the opportunities that had been afforded to her as the result of being a Breton speaker:

> *Ma vefen ket brezongerez sur eo zo traou 'mefe ket greet gwech ebed, evel: mond d'ar festou-noz, kaout eun toullad mignoned er skol-veur, studial e Bro-Gembre, ha kemer perz en eun tamm asosiasion, ober eun tamm teatr, kana gand eur strollad mignonezed, ha dre ze kemer perz e festou zo, gwiska dillad ma mamm-guñv evid eured magerez ma mab n'eus ket pell zo …*

> (If I weren't a Breton speaker, it's likely there are certain activities I would never have done, such as: going to festoù-noz, meeting many new friends at university, studying in Wales, taking part in a number of cultural associations, doing some drama, singing in an all-female choir and then taking part in festivals, wearing my mother-in-law's traditional costume for my son's marriage which recently took place …) (Plourin-Yviquel, 2009, p. 17)

Incorporating the idea that Breton is language like any other, one Breton speaker said: 'Re aliez e soñj din e vez greet eur yez sakr deus ar brezoneg' (I think that, too often, Breton is made out to be a 'sacred' language) (Gouvres, 2009, p. 29), indicating that linguistic practices, and not speakers, can be privileged in some discourses. The three Breton speakers above show more positive attitudes towards the language, arising out of ideologies which place the speaker/language user at the heart of discourses, rather than the language itself; as Le Nevez has suggested, there is a need for 'understanding Breton not as a language but as a range of situated social practices [which] will likely lead to initiatives that are not focused on the language but on the language community' (Le Nevez, 2013, p. 98).

Ideological opposition to language revitalisation

It might be imagined that attempts to breathe fresh life into a language undergoing attrition would be universally welcomed. However, the literature shows that there is much ideological opposition to the idea that the language in question should be revitalised. Writers such as McDonald (1989), Jones (1998) and Le Dû and Le Berre (2013) have documented the existence of an apparent gap between older and younger generations of Breton speakers. Lossec, in an interview in 2013 ('Bretons', 83, p. 41), has summed up the ideological tension which can lead to the delegitimisation of new speakers of Breton:

> Moi, ce qui m'énerve le plus, ce sont les gens qui disent: ce n'est pas le même breton. Ce sont des anciens, on a l'impression que le breton est à eux, qu'ils n'ont pas d'envie de le partager. Alors dès qu'il y a un mot mal prononcé, ou un peu mal dit, ou un petit mot qu'ils n'ont pas entendu, c'est tout de suite ça.

> (What I get most annoyed about are those people who say: it isn't the same Breton [as they speak]. So when a word is badly pronounced, or said awkwardly, or there's a word which [these people] have not come across before, then they resort to this.)

This divide has been commented upon in interviews I have conducted with Breton speakers, and which I have reported on in particular in Hornsby (2015):

> My neighbour who is over eighty years old doesn't want to speak to me. She trots out a couple of words (of Breton) sometimes, and then when I answer back in Breton, she wriggles out of the conversation: 'Well, yes, you've learned *good* Breton … but it's just not the same … ' (Hornsby, 2015, p. 56; emphasis added)

Thus, even though the research participant's neighbour seemingly compliments her level of Breton as being 'good', the subtext is that her Breton is not 'authentic' enough, because she uses standard Breton, as opposed to the local dialect. This is a common enough situation in many instances of language minoritisation. What has been less reported on is in-group ideological opposition where new speakers jostle for positions of authenticity in relation to each other. O'Rourke and Walsh found in Ireland that new speakers engage in language policing with each other (O'Rourke & Walsh, 2015, p. 74), whereby new speakers ensure that notions of language authenticity are maintained as an in-group norm. O'Rourke and Ramallo (2013) found similar behaviour among new speakers in Galicia where 'new speakers' sanctioning and policing of each other through purist linguistic attitudes also point to a strongly essentialist bias about language, where clear linguistic boundaries need to be adhered to' (O'Rourke & Ramallo, 2013, p. 31).

An example of this linguistic policing of new speakers in a Breton context can be found in Hewitt (in press). Here, Hewitt, discussing the lack of a consensus over an acceptable orthography for all users of Breton, diverges from matters orthographic sensu stricto, and expresses discontent when new speakers transgress certain linguistic boundaries. He ascribes purism to new speakers' lexical choices, since the neologisms they are purported to use are 'quite opaque to traditional speakers' (Hewitt, in press), indulging in what he terms 'lexical xenophobia' (Hewitt, in press). Furthermore, new speakers have

'French phonetic habits (and) little idea of Breton idiom or phraseology. Their syntax is either calqued on French or hypercorrectly different from French ... ' (Hewitt, in press). New speakers of Breton, as a group, are sweepingly contrasted with 'real native speakers', who use 'spontaneous Breton', and who find the speech of new speakers 'upsetting', since it 'in no way resembles the living language of traditional native speakers' (Hewitt, in press). The suggestion is that 'the only form of Breton that is likely to persist, in small networks of aficionados, is that of the learner-activist neo-speakers' (Hewitt, in press). What is apparent, in this commentator's view, is that new speakers, as a speaker category, consistently fail to reach a certain benchmark and therefore their linguistic practices are to be discounted as being 'inauthentic'. In contrast to his accusation of 'lexical xenophobia', we might note on his part an ideology based on phonocentrism (among other native speaker-based centrisms), much along the lines described by Chow, in which 'ideologically loaded phenomena such as accents and intonations' (Chow, 2014, p. 11) are used to discredit the linguistic practices of those new speakers who are not as proficient, or as confident, or who lack the same opportunities for acquiring Breton linguistic resources, as the commentator. That the author is himself a new speaker of Breton suggests that this is a clear case of in-group linguistic policing, in which lines are drawn between 'them' (new speakers) and 'us' (native speakers and their supporters), a position which Quentel and I have described elsewhere as 'native authenticists' (Hornsby & Quentel, 2013, p. 78).

Overt ideologies in action: postvernacular practices

New speakers of Breton, then, sometimes have to deal with negative attitudes towards their linguistic practices. One of the ways they do this is by adopting overt ideologies of language which lead to positive attitudes which act as a counter-balance to the negativity they are sometimes subjected to. As a result, they engage in practices which they personally find validating, even if these same practices are rejected as 'inauthentic' by other speakers and commentators. A number of interviews conducted for a recent edition of 'Bretons' (111, 2015) revealed a wide range of non-traditional linguistic practices which could be generally described as 'postvernacular', in the sense that they are located in non-traditional domains and which these new speakers have developed and which advance the Breton language which were not considered permissible or even 'appropriate' in previous generations. Jahier (2015, p. 30), for example, had to confront such attitudes from former colleagues when she learned Breton as part of a career change: 'There were people who had certain agendas ... I had to put up with quite a lot of criticism from former colleagues. They would say to me: You're a bit crazy, [learning Breton] is useless' (*Il y a des gens qui ont des a priori ... J'ai essuyé pas mal de critiques d'anciens collègues. Ils me disaient : T'es un peu folle, ça ne sert à rien*). Another interviewee, Coatanlem (2015, p. 27), who became a new speaker of Breton through immersion schooling, noted that her parents' motivation in placing her in an immersion school was not linguistic, but pragmatic; immersion schools in Brittany (Diwan) have smaller classes than public ones (*Mes parents m'y ont inscrite (à Diwan) parce que, contrairement à l'école publique, il y avait de petits effectifs. Ce n'était pas pour le breton ...*). Seeing education in Breton as being advantageous to a child is a very different attitude from the attitudes of previous generations, especially for most of the twentieth century, when Breton speakers sent their children to the local school, knowing full well that their children would be 'transformed' into monolingual French speakers. This attitude towards Breton is prevalent only among a small minority of parents in Brittany, but for the situation to arise when parents could even begin to consider Breton-language education for their children is located in postvernacular ideologies of language, after most of the population of Brittany had shifted to French. It is only now, in a postvernacular mode, that Breton can be considered appropriate as an educational (or workplace) language. Coatanlem (2015, p. 27) further points out that she had trouble convincing her family from outside Brittany that Breton was a bone fide, modern language; they only accepted her legitimacy as a Breton speaker after she found work where Breton was the working language: 'Since I found work, I've seen the change [in them] ... they no longer tell me it's a dead language!' (*Depuis que j'ai trouvé du travail, j'ai vraiment vu le changement ... ils ne me disent plus que c'est une langue morte!*)

This is part of a process Pentecouteau (2002) has referred to as 'secondary socialization', which comes after primary socialisation (within the family) and which he says consists of 'accessing a new system of references which is constructed as part of the process, but without making a clean slate of the first system of references' (Pentecouteau, 2002, p. 113; my translation). In other words, new speakers of Breton were (in general) primarily socialised in French before becoming new speakers of Breton and this marks them as 'different' in many ways from previous generations of Breton speakers. Breton-language networks are increasingly constructed and maintained by new speakers and thus the language, as it moves out of traditionally vernacular domains, is becoming postvernacular, both in form and in practice.

Conclusion

The postvernacularisation of Breton, occurring in a situation of language shift, has come about because of the restriction in the domains where it can be used, and commentators such as Bentahila and Davies note that,

> it is extremely difficult if not impossible to persuade people en masse (as opposed to the occasional intellectual) to use a language in contexts where they do not really need it, or to enforce its intergenerational transfer on any large scale. (Bentahila & Davies, 1993, p. 372)

They conclude that transformation is a much more realistic prospect for many threatened languages: 'the production of reasonably accomplished non-native speakers, the standardization of the language or the provision for it to be used in new domains seem to be much more accessible goals' (Bentahila & Davies, 1993, p. 372). Thus, the appearance of recent social and linguistic practices, in which some (but not all) speakers of Breton innovate and transform the language that has been transmitted to them in alternative ways other than intergenerational transmission, is hardly surprising. As Breton develops within contemporary networks of varied linguistic practices, it is acquiring features associated with new speakers. Moving away from its traditional domains of use, where it is used vernacularly (but less so), Breton is becoming a 'postvernacular' language in many respects, which as we have seen, can be seen in positive terms, depending on the language ideologies held by contemporary speakers and commentators. That these transformations are not always seen positively, from a variety of ideological perspectives, is also symptomatic of the process of postvernacularisation.

Acknowledgements

An earlier version of this article was given as an invited contribution to the First Celtic Sociolinguistics Symposium at University College Dublin, 24–26 June 2015. The writing of this article has furthermore benefitted from ongoing discussions on the themes of 'new speakers' as part of the COST EU Action IS1306 entitled, 'New Speakers in a Multilingual Europe: Opportunities and Challenges'. The author wishes to thank three anonymous reviewers for their suggestions on the content and structure of the present article.

ORCiD

Michael Hornsby ⓘ http://orcid.org/0000-0002-6075-5929

References

Abalain, H. (1989). *Destin des langues celtiques* [The destiny of the Celtic languages]. Paris: OPHRYS.
Armstrong, T. C. (2012). Establishing new norms of language use: The circulation of linguistic ideology in three new Irish-language communities. *Language Policy, 11*, 145–168.
Beer, H. (2009). Yiddish without Yiddish? *European Judaism, 42*(2), 10–18.
Bentahila, A., & Davies, E. (1993). Language revival: Restoration or transformation? *Journal of Multilingual and Multicultural Development, 14*(5), 355–374.
Blech, B. (2000). *The complete idiot's guide to learning Yiddish*. Indianapolis, IN: Alpha Books.
Broudic, F. (1995). *La pratique du breton de l'ancien régime à nos jours* [The practice of Breton-speaking from the pre-Revolutionary period to the present time]. Rennes: Presses Universitaires de Rennes.
Chow, R. (2014). *Not like a native speaker. On languaging as a postcolonial experience*. New York, NY: Columbia University Press.
Cléac'h, F. (2015). *Le Sale Petit Breton. Années de pensionat en Cornouaille (1947–1954)* [The dirty little Breton. Years at boarding school in South-West Brittany (1947–1954)]. Fouesnant: Yoran Embaner.
Coatanlem, O. 2015. Plus personne ne me dit que le breton est une langue morte [No longer does anyone say to me that Breton is a dead language]. *Bretons, 111*, 27.
Costa, J. (2015). New speakers, new language: On being a legitimate speaker of a minority language in Provence. *International Journal of the Sociology of Language, 231*, 127–145.
Dickinson, J. (2010). Languages for the market, the nation, or the margins: Overlapping ideologies of language and identity in Zakarpattia. *International Journal of the Sociology of Language, 201*, 53–78.
Dorian, N. C. (1986). Making do with less: Some surprises along the language death proficiency continuum. *Applied Psycholinguistics, 7*, 257–276.
Dorian, N. C. (1999). The study of language obsolescence: Stages, surprises, and challenges. *Languages and Linguistics, 3*, 99–122.
Edwards, J. (2004). Language, diversity and identity. In J. Edwards (Ed.), *Linguistic minorities, policies and pluralism: Applied language studies* (pp. 277–310). London: Academic Press.
Glazer, N. (1980). Towards a sociology of small ethnic groups, a discourse and discussion. *Canadian Ethnic Studies, 12*, 1–16.
Gouvres, Y.-H. (2009). Ar brezoneg n'eo ket eur yez sakr [Breton isn't a sacred language]. *Brud Nevez, 277*, 27–29.

SUPPORT, TRANSMISSION, EDUCATION AND TARGET VARIETIES

Grenoble, L. A., & Whaley, L. J. (Eds.) (1998). *Endangered languages: Current issues and future prospects*. Cambridge: Cambridge University Press.

Heaton, J. (2014). *Reworking qualitative data*. London: Sage.

Heller, M. (2003). Globalization, the new economy, and the commodification of language and identity. *Journal of Sociolinguistics, 7*, 473–492.

Hewitt, S. (in press). Breton orthographies. An increasingly awkward fit. In M. C. Jones & D. Mooney (Eds.), *Orthography development for endangered languages*. Cambridge: Cambridge University Press.

Hornsby, M. (2015). *Revitalizing minority languages: New speakers of Breton, Yiddish and Lemko*. Basingstoke: Palgrave Macmillan.

Hornsby, M., & Quentel, G. (2013). Contested varieties and competing authenticities: Neologisms in revitalised Breton. *International Journal of the Sociology of Language, 223*, 71–86.

Hornsby, M., & Vigers, D. (2013). Breton: The postvernacular challenge. *International Journal of the Sociology of Language, 223*, 1–6.

Irvine, J. T. (1989). When talk isn't cheap: Language and political economy. *American Ethnologist, 16*, 248–267.

Jahier, S. (2015). Maintenant, je parle à mes petits-enfants en breton [I now talk Breton to my grandchildren]. *Bretons, 111*, 30.

Jones, M. C. (1998). *Language obsolescence and revitalization. Linguistic change in two sociolinguistically contrasting Welsh communities*. Oxford: Oxford University Press.

Katz, D. (2015). *Yiddish and power*. London: Palgrave MacMillan.

Kroskrity, P. (2004). Language ideology. In A. Duranti (Ed.), *Companion to linguistic anthropology* (pp. 496–517). Oxford: Blackwell.

Le Dû, J., & Le Berre, Y. (2013). La langue bretonne dans la société régionale contemporaine [The Breton language in the contemporary regional society]. *International Journal of the Sociology of Language, 223*, 43–54.

Le Nevez, A. (2013). The social practice of Breton. An epistemological challenge. *International Journal of the Sociology of Language, 223*, 87–102.

Le Pipec, E. (2013). Les trois ruptures sociolinguistiques du breton [The three sociolinguistic breaks in Breton]. *International Journal of the Sociology of Language, 223*, 103–116.

McDonald, M. (1989). *We are not French! Language, culture and identity in Brittany*. London: Routledge.

Mertz, E. (1989). Sociolinguistic creativity. Cape Breton Gaelic's linguistic "tip". In N. C. Dorian (Ed.), *Investigating obsolescence. Studies in language contraction and death* (pp. 103–116). Cambridge: Cambridge University Press.

Mufwene, S. S. (2004). Language birth and death. *Annual Review of Anthropology, 33*, 201–222.

Naoueg, T. (2009). Perag emaon o pellaad deus ar brezoneg? [Why am I distancing myself from Breton?]. *Brud Nevez, 277*, 30–31.

Ó hIfearnáin, T. (2014). Paradoxes of engagement with Irish language community management, practice and ideology. In P. K. Austin & J. Sallabank (Eds.), *Endangered languages: Beliefs and ideologies in language documentation and revitalization* (pp. 29–51). Oxford: Oxford University Press.

O'Rourke, B., & Ramallo, F. (2013). Competing ideologies of linguistic authority amongst new speakers in contemporary Galicia. *Language in Society, 42*(3), 287–305.

O'Rourke, B., & Walsh, J. (2015). New speakers of Irish: Shifting boundaries across time and space. *International Journal of the Sociology of Language, 231*, 63–83.

Pentecouteau, H. (2002). *Devenir bretonnant : Découvertes, apprentissages et réappropriations d'une langue* [Becoming a Breton speaker: Discoveries, learning and reappropriation of a language]. Rennes: Presses Universitaires de Rennes.

Plourin-Yviquel, G. (2009). Vous l'avez appris à l'école… [You learnt it at school…]. *Brud Nevez, 277*, 16–17.

Sallabank, J. (2013). *Attitudes to endangered languages. Identities and policies*. Cambridge: Cambridge University Press.

Shandler, J. (2004). Postvernacular Yiddish: Language as a performance art. *TDR/The Drama Review, 48*(1), 19–43.

SUPPORT, TRANSMISSION, EDUCATION AND TARGET VARIETIES

Shandler, J. (2006). *Adventures in Yiddishland: Postvernacular language and culture*. Oakland: University of California Press.

Texier, M., & Ó Néill, D. (2000). *The Nominoë study of the Breton language*. Retrieved from http://www.breizh.nwt/icdbl/saozg/nominoe.htm

Thieberger, N. (2002). Extinction in whose terms? In D. Bradley & M. Bradley (Eds.), *Language endangerment and language maintenance: An active approach* (pp. 310–328). London: Curzon.

Tulloch, S. (2006). Preserving dialects of an endangered language. *Current Issues in Language Planning, 7*(2–3), 269–286.

Woolard, K., & Schieffelin, B. (1994). Language ideology. *Annual Review of Anthropology, 23*, 55–82.

Index

Note: **Boldface** page numbers refer to tables, page numbers followed by "n" denote endnotes

Abalain, H. 95
'activist' framework 94
additive bilingualism 77–8
Adventures in Yiddishland (Shandler) 93
Armstrong, T. C. 96
autobiographies 95–6

Baker, C. 7, 51; bilingual education framework 48–9, 52, 55–6; Gaelic-medium education 55–6
BBC Alba 16–17
Béal Bocht, An (O'Nolan) 20
Beer, H. 94
Bentahila, A. 8, 101
bilingual education: Baker's framework 7, 48–9, 52, 55–6; as language planning 56, 68; as pedagogy 48, 55; as politics 49, 55–6; programmes 5
Bilingual Education Project 34
bilingualism 24–5, 76–7; additive 77–8; flexible 87; hybrid 92; subtractive 77
Blech, B. 93
Blommaert, J. 78
Bonfiglio, T. 77
Bòrd na Gàidhlig 17, 26n5
Breton 14–16, 92–3; case of 95; modernisation of 98; new speakers of 97–9, 101; in postvernacular mode 93, 101; speakers 92, 96, 98, 99; spontaneous 100
Breton: The Postvernacular Challenge (Hornsby & Vigers) 93
Brittany: French in 96, 101; language shift in 95; speaker demographics 2
Broudic, F. 95
Bun-sgoil Ghaidhlig Inbhir Nis 16
Bun-sgoil Shlèite 16

Caimbeul, Dòmhnall 17
Canada, language setting in 2, 91–2
Canagarajah, S. 78

Celtic language-medium education 4
Celtic languages 13–14; alternative modes of transmission 3; Breton 14–16; Cornish 14–16; current status and future trajectories 4; discursive framing of 4, 5; education in 5–7; fostering support 3–4; Gaelic 16–17; growth of 14; institutionalisation of 6; 'Insular', notion of 1, 9n1; Irish-language 17–21; loss of status and prestige 3; maintenance of 14; Manx 14–16; minoritisation and language shift 1; 'new speakers' 8; official and semi-official agencies 23; proficiency in 6; social use of 33; sociolinguistics of 1, 4; speaker demographics 2–3; target varieties for 8–9; understanding of 2; Welsh 14–16
Celtic Sociolinguistics Symposium 1
Cléac'h, F. 96
Coatanlem, O. 100, 101
code-switching 41, 77, 79
Committee on Irish Language Attitudes Research (1975) 18, 19
complete idiot's guide to learning Yiddish, The (Blech) 93
Comunn Gàidhealach, An 17
Cornish 2, 14–16
Costa, J. 93
covert ideologies of language 92
Cré na Cille (Ó Cadhain) 19
cultural-linguistic framework 92
Cummins, J. 77

Dauenhauer, N. M. 42
Dauenhauer, R. 42
Davies, E. 8, 101
Day, Jon 19, 21
Delivering Equality of Opportunity in Schools (DEIS) 83
diglossia, notion of 78, 81
Dirty Dust, The (Titley) 19
Dirty Little Breton, The (Cléac'h) 96
Dòmhnullach, A. 17
Dorian, N. 23, 91
double monolingualism 78

INDEX

double-standard, concept of 39–41
Dunn, C. 21
dynamic process of langugaing 78

Edwards, J. 3–4, 14, 15, 21, 93
Eichler, W. 16
English 1; in BBC Alba 16; dominance 3, 17; in Gaelic-medium education context 34; 'Irishising' of 82; Maggie's case 35, 36, 39, 42; translation works 19–20, 27n15; Will's suggestion 35
Evans, D. 15

Fishman, J. 18, 32
fixed language categories 77
Flores, N. 82
fluid process of langugaing 78
French 1; in Brittany 96, 101; dominance 3; phonetic habits 100; speakers, in Ontario 92

Gaelic: child-directed uses of 5; de-normatising 39–41; double-standard, concept of 40; in education 55–6, 60–2, **61**, 62, 68–9; exposure to 54, 57–8, **58**, 65, 74–5; Family Language Policy 36; future of 55, 59–60, **60**, 64; in Isle of Skye 34; language planning 56; language programming 16–17; linguistic competence 34; 'monolingual Gaelic' 36, 41, 44n3; as performance language 36–9; speaker demographics 2–3; third generation's use of 36; value of learning 55–6; see also Scottish Gaelic
Gaelic medium education (GME) 34–5, 42–3, 71n2; Baker's framework 55–6; binary logistic regression 56; cross-party-political support 50; cultural and national identities 54–5, 58–9, **59**, 75; demographic factors 54, 56–7, **57**, 74; dependent variable 53; 'dimensions of interest' 51; education-based rationales 50; exposure to Gaelic 54, 57–8, **58**, 65, 74–5; future of Gaelic 55, 59–60, **60**, 64; 'Gaelic in education' dimension 55–6, 60–2, **61**, 62, 68–9; growth of 49; implications and limitations 70–1; importance of 71n1; likelihood of choice 51, **51**, 62, **63–4**, 65–7, 69, 70; linguistic and cultural heritage-based rationales 50; logistic regression model 67; methodological approach 67–8; 1980 Education Act 49; 1981 Education Act 49; parental choice of 49–52; research questions 52; in Scotland 7, 49–50, 70; Scottish Index of Multiple Deprivation 66, 71n4; Scottish Social Attitudes Survey (2012) 51–3; 2016 Education Act 50; type II tests of deviance 56, 62, **64**
Gaeltacht 14, 21, 23
Gàidhealtachd 14
García, O. 79
GME see Gaelic medium education

Gorter, D. 79
Gort, M. 78
Graded Intergenerational Disruption Scale 32

Hansen, M. 15
Heaton, J. 95–6
Heller, M. 78, 92
Hewitt, S. 99
Hornberger, N. 82
Hornsby, M. 8, 14, 99
hybrid bilingualism 92
hybrid language use 80, 81

ideological opposition: to language revitalisation 99–100; new speakers of Breton and 97–9
ideology of language 92
immersion language education 32–3, 49, 100
'Insular' Celtic varieties 1, 9n1
integrative ethnographic approach 83
Ireland, language setting in 2
Irish language 7, 17–21; bottom-up language policy 82; context 79–80; education system 81–3; ideological and implementational spaces 82, 87; positioning of 82; revitalisation 87; speakers 81; speech community 82; teaching experience 84–5
Irish Language Survey (2013) 70

Johnson, D. C. 82
Jones, M. C. 95, 97, 99
Jørgensen, J. N. 77, 78

Katz, D. 94
Kelly, A. 82
Kelly-Holmes, H. 78
Kiberd, Declan 19–21, 28n16
King, K. A. 42

language codes 77
Language, Culture and Curriculum 1
language ideologies 92
language maintenance 5, 7, 61, 80
language management 4, 8
language policy, in Ireland 23, 81–3, 87
language revitalisation 80, 97, 99–100
language shift; reversing language shift: in Brittany 95; Dorian's suggestion 91; postvernacularisation 93–5; role of language ideologies 92; see also ideological opposition
Le Berre, Y. 99
Le Dû, J. 99
Lemke, J. 77
Le Pipec, E. 98
lexical xenophobia 99–100
'life stories' 95–6
linguistic policing 99, 100

INDEX

MacDonald, A. 17
Macdonell, H. 16
Mac Gréil, M. 18, 19, 25
MacKenzie, K. 16, 17
MacLeod, M. 17
MacNamara, John 32–3
MacNeacail, A. 17
Maggie's case 5, 33; Campbell family 34; de-normatising Gaelic 39–41; double-standard, concept of 40; 'free breaks' 35; Gaelic as performance language 36–9; Gaelic medium education 34, 42–3; implications for education in RLS 32, 41–4; language use 35; micro-interactional analysis 5, 35–6; 'monolingual Gaelic' 36, 41, 44n3; sociocultural landscape 35; Will's hypothesis 34
Mahaffy, John 21
Makropoulos, J. 71
Manx 14–16
McDonald, M. 99
Mertz, E. 91
metrolingualism 78
micro-interactional analysis 5, 35–6
minority language: academic literature on 3; Breton case 95; in education 5; European context 87; immersion education 33; immersion programmes 5; levels of support 9; rap as translanguaging resource 80–1; revitalisation 80; social use of 33; teaching of 80; translanguaging and 77–8, 80–1
Møller, J. S. 77, 78
'monolingual Gaelic' 36, 41, 44n3
monolingualism 24, 78, 87
Moriarty, Máiréad 7
Mufwene, S. S. 95

'new speakers' 8; of Breton 97–9, 101

O'Brien, Flann 19, 20
Observer's Paradox 41–2
Ó Cadhain, Máirtín 19–20
Ó Caollaí, Maolsheachlainn 19
Ó Criomhthain, Tomás 20, 27n13
Ó Danachair, C. 21
Ó Giollagáin, C. 23
Ó hIfearnáin, T. 8, 14, 15, 26n2, 96
O'Malley-Madec, M. 82
Ó Murchú, M. 82
1872 Education Act 34
O'Nolan, Brian 19, 20
Ontario, minority French speakers in 92
O'Rourke, B. 81, 99
Otheguy, R. 79
overt ideologies of language 92, 94, 100–1

parallel monolingualism 77, 78, 87
Pennycook, A. 80

Pentecouteau, H. 101
performance language, Gaelic as 36–9
polylanguaging 78
postvernacularisation 100–1; and language shift 93–5
pro-minority language ideologies 42
Puigdevall, M. 81
Pujolar, J. 81

Ramallo, F. 99
rap as translanguaging resource 80–1; language diversity **84**; pedagogic resource 83; pupils' experience **84**, 85–6, **86**; rules for 85, **85**; teacher's experience 84–5, **85**
Reid, W. 79
reversing language shift (RLS) 32; implications for education 41–4
Robertson, Boyd 16
Romaine, S. 8
Russell, Bertrand 21

Sabhal Mòr Ostaig 16
Sallabank, J. 15, 16, 93
Schissel, J. L. 82
Scotland: Bun-sgoil Ghaidhlig Inbhir Nis 16; Bun-sgoil Shlèite 16; Gaelic speakers in 71n5; 1980 Education Act 49; 1981 Education Act 49; 2016 Education Act 50
Scottish Gaelic: in education 34–5; lack of use 5; speaker demographics 2–3; *see also* Gaelic
Scottish Index of Multiple Deprivation (SIMD) 66, 71n4
Scottish Social Attitudes Survey (2012) 7, 51–3
'secondary analysis' approach 95
'secondary socialization' 101
second-language teaching 7
Sembiante, S. F. 78
Shandler, J.: *Adventures in Yiddishland* 93; postvernacularity 93–4
SIMD *see* Scottish Index of Multiple Deprivation
Smith-Christmas, C. 5, 37
social use of minority language 33
Spolsky, B. 32
subtractive bilingualism 77

Thieberger, N. 97
Titley, Alan 19
translanguaging 79; bilingualism 77–8; classroom context 83; Gorter, D. 79; and Irish language pedagogy 79–80; linguistic and cultural resources 80–1; metrolingualism 78; multilingualism 77–8; pedagogic resource for 76, 83–6; pedagogy 7; polylanguaging 78; rap 80–1, **84–6**, 85–6; Williams, C. 79; *see also* minority language
'truncated competence' 80
Tulloch, S. 80, 95

INDEX

Walsh, J. 81, 99
Wei, L. 79
Welsh language 14–16
Welsh-medium education 48, 68
Williams, C. 79
Will's hypothesis 34

Ya d'ar brezhoneg ('Yes to Breton') campaign 15
Yiddish: 'postvernacular' 94; Shandler's
reference to 93, 94